W A Y S I D E
Revelations

by Roy Wilson Henry

Foreword by Dwight R. Platt

Introduction by Robert M. Schrag

*To Dam and Trevye Graber,
Love,
Roy Wilson Henry*

☀ **Wordsworth – Newton, Kansas**

Library of Congress Catalog Card Number 94-61730

ISBN 0-945530-12-9

Wayside Revelations appeared previously in a slightly different version in semimonthly columns by Roy W. Henry published from 1976 to 1994 in *Mennonite Weekly Review*.

Unless otherwise noted, scripture references are from the Revised Standard Version of *The Holy Bible*, 1952.

Cover by Steve Banman
Line drawing illustrations in text by Carolyn Urich
Back cover photograph of Roy Henry by Anna Kreider Juhnke

Computer-generated typesetting by Wordsworth

Printed in the United States of America by Pine Hill Press, Freeman, South Dakota

This book is printed on recycled ♺ and acid-free ∞ paper.

To my wife,

Glennys Alene Kaufman Henry,

for her patience through days and weeks of separation
while I snooped around on and off trails
and "no trails"
in prairies, mountains, deserts,
and other "ordinary" fascinating places.

Acknowledgments

First, I want to express my appreciation to Robert M. Schrag, editor of *Mennonite Weekly Review*, where the columns and photographs of this book were first published. Robert's positive support for my columns throughout the years has been very helpful.

It has been a pleasure to work with LaVonne Platt, my editor at Wordsworth. She was very thorough in editing, as well as being flexible and encouraging all along the way.

I want to thank Laura Cossey, who helped LaVonne by entering the manuscript on computer and by making layout changes and corrections, always with good humor and generosity in scheduling her time to meet deadlines. Her expertise was much appreciated.

I am grateful to Steve Banman for the cover design. He contributed greatly to make the outside of the book convey the message I intended on the inside pages.

Bluffton artist Carolyn Sauder Urich also lent her skills to the book by preparing the sketches for the section pages which introduce each season's columns. I thank her for sharing her work.

Through the years of writing nature columns, I have benefited greatly in taking and developing photographs from the helpful suggestions of my son Lyle, who has been my teacher in the technical aspects of photography. His guidance has been invaluable to me.

I appreciate the support of members of Bluffton Creative Writers Fellowship, and I especially thank Elaine Sommers Rich for the encouragement and support she gave me in this project.

My thanks, too, for delightful and informative stays with members of "Mennonite Your Way" and other friends in whose homes I visited through the years. I enjoyed the companionship of those who accompanied me on many a trail and path. I learned much from those who shared their stories of the out-of-doors; their interest encouraged me to continue to share my experiences as I studied and enjoyed God's fascinating creation.

Most of all I wish to thank Glennys for her support, for "keeping the home fires burning" through my sometimes lengthy journeys researching material for my writings.

—Roy Wilson Henry

About the Author

Early in his life, Roy Wilson Henry developed an avid interest in nature. As a child growing up with three brothers and three sisters on a farm near Gypsum Creek in Saline County, Kansas, his home life and his playtime often centered around his family's interests in the animals and plants that were a part of their environment.

Roy's mother, Myrtle Mahala Morris Henry, had a special interest in birds and enjoyed "translating" bird songs into words that mimicked the sound, helping her children remember the songs of the different species of birds they often heard. Roy's father, Edward Thomas Henry, built bird houses for wrens, chickadees, and other birds, using materials such as hollow logs and axle-grease cans, and installed them near the Henry home. Roy delighted in watching the progress of the bird families that nested in the bird houses and other sites on the farmstead and along Gypsum Creek. By the time Roy was ten or eleven, he and his brothers and sisters knew where to find most of the nests in the area.

Exploring along the creek, digging into the banks to probe out roots in the sandy loam soil, and building wigwams with tall stalks of sunflowers woven with fresh alfalfa were among the activities Roy and his siblings enjoyed when they were children.

After completing eight grades in the rural Bridgehall School, Roy helped his father on the farm for four years and then moved to Mentor, Kansas, where he lived with his Uncle William and Aunt Vera Henry and their family so that he could attend Smolan High School. Later he graduated from Bethel College in North Newton, Kansas, and Bethany Seminary in Chicago, Illinois.

Roy has taught in elementary schools and high schools in Kansas and Ohio, as well as in the Academia Bautista at Barrenquitas, Puerto Rico. He participated in Civilian Public Service in Colorado Springs, Colorado, where he worked with the Soil Conservation Service. He was Director of Swiss Farm Outdoor Education Center at Bluffton College in Ohio, and taught courses in Outdoor Education, Conservation, Outdoor Recreation, and Camping. He was a summer naturalist at Beaver Creek State Park in Ohio and has served as a nature resource leader for campers of all ages at numerous church camps in Kansas, Colorado, Michigan, and several other states.

He served as pastor at Mennonite churches in Burrton, Kansas; Hillsboro, Kansas; Topeka, Indiana; and Wadsworth, Ohio. For three years was chaplain at Meadowlark Homestead in Newton, Kansas. For several years he was a social worker at Allen County Department of Welfare in Lima, Ohio.

He has traveled widely on field trips to study nature throughout the United States, and other countries, including Canada, Mexico, Nicaragua, Virgin Islands, Cuba, Haiti, and Dominican Republic. He participated in a United Nations Relief and Reconstruction Agency project to ship horses to Poland after World War II.

From 1971 to 1984, Roy Henry wrote a weekly column, "Outdoor Panorama" for his hometown newspaper, the *Bluffton News*. For about 10 years he also wrote a column describing his boyhood in central Kansas. Titled "Gadding About Gypsum Creek," the column of reminiscenses appeared in the *Gypsum Advocate* section of the *Lindsborg News Record* approximately once a month.

Since 1976, Roy has been a columnist for *Mennonite Weekly Review,* published in Newton, Kansas. He has selected more than five dozen favorite "Wayside Revelations" columns that previously appeared in *Mennonite Weekly Review* to form the text of this book. Photographs that Roy took on his many explorations of nature and later developed in his home darkroom illustrate the columns and the book.

Roy and his wife, Glennys, were married in 1945. They have lived in Bluffton, Ohio, since 1967. They had four children—Lyle, Carol, Larry, and Mona. Lyle and his family also live in Bluffton. Mona lives in Columbus, Ohio. After Larry's death in 1990 and after Carol's death in 1993, Roy shared some of his memories about their lives in "Wayside Revelations" columns that are included in this book.

Foreword

There are some who can live without wild things, and some who cannot. These essays are the delights and dilemmas of one who cannot.
—Aldo Leopold, *A Sand County Almanac*

Aldo Leopold's words in the Foreword to *A Sand County Almanac*, could also be applied to this book and to its author. Roy Wilson Henry is also a person who finds delight in nature and its wild things. He is one of the persons described by Leopold for whom "the opportunity to see geese is more important than television, and the chance to find a pasque-flower is a right as inalienable as free speech."

Roy has served in a number of occupations—as minister, teacher, social worker, administrator—but his life-long vocation is an interpreter of nature. He was a pioneer in nature education and recreation before such activities enjoyed the popularity they have today. He has inspired many to an appreciation of God's creation.

I first met Roy Henry almost 50 years ago in the 1940s when he was a student at Bethel College and I was a high school student at Newton growing up near the college campus. I spent much time hiking along Sand Creek near Newton observing nature, especially trying to identify birds with the few books I had available. When I met Roy, he introduced me to Peterson's *Field Guide to the Birds* which made identifcation of birds much easier.

But more important, I found someone who shared a common interest in the natural world. I have many memories of bird hikes with Roy, when, after stalking the "chip" coming out of the plum thicket ahead, he helped me identify the confusing sparrow or warbler. On a cold December day in 1949, along with my cousin Jim Rich, we hiked along Sand Creek and started the traditional count of winter birds which has continued as the Halstead-Newton Christmas Bird Count. In the summer of 1950, Roy and I traveled together to the Audubon Nature Camp in Kerrville, Texas, and then on south to Big Bend National Park. Roy's willingness to share his enthusiastic interest in and familiarity with nature was an inspiration in the development of my own interest.

Roy Henry has a rich legacy of persons who, like myself, have been inspired on a nature hike, at a camp, or by his nature columns in *Mennonite Weekly Review,* and who have gone on to develop an interest in nature that has enriched their lives. With an insatiable curiosity about animals and plants, he has stimulated that curiosity in others.

Now with the publication of this book, Roy Wilson Henry leaves a more permanent written legacy that should inspire all of us to appreciate and take care of the living world which surrounds us.

−Dwight R. Platt
Professor of Biology, Bethel College
North Newton, Kansas

Introduction

Finding Wonder in the Commonplace

Shakespeare, writing of the fabled forest of Arden, declares that a person attuned to nature's message can find "tongues in trees, books in running brooks, sermons in stones, and good in everything." The description fits Roy Wilson Henry. He combines the knowledge of a natural science teacher, the experience of a veteran field observer, and the writing skill of an essayist. Moreover, he views the natural world through the lens of Christian faith.

Since 1976 the editors of *Mennonite Weekly Review* have had the privilege of publishing the author's twice-monthly column, "Wayside Revelations," from which the chapters of this book are selected. Through his writing he has taken his readers on a continuing survey of nature's wonders and whims, its patterns and peculiarities.

From the woods and streams near his home in Bluffton, Ohio, he has ranged across North America, meticulously recording his observations of fauna and flora in widely differing environments. He describes with equal skill and enthusiasm the antics of a pet mouse or the awesome sight of a whale breaching along the Pacific coast.

Henry's essays truly are revelations, bringing to light obscure details and fascinating aspects of creation's seemingly endless variety. Mother Nature is revealed in all seasons, in many places and in a vast array of guises—the drama of a late-winter ice breakup on an Ohio creek; the familiar call of a whip-poor-will mimicked by a mockingbird atop a Kansas silo; the nocturnal thievery of raccoons at a Texas campsite.

With frequent touches of humor, his vignettes of wildlife often depict the denizens of tree and meadow as individuals with almost human characteristics. The reader is introduced to Woody the wood frog, Heecliff the dove and Tommy woodpecker. A bird trying vainly to fly off with a securely fastened piece of twine becomes "a modern robin Don Quixote challenging a wire fence." The croaking of frogs is transformed into "a concert steeped in the ancient toadlore of a venerable race." An ordinary bird feeder may be an "avian smorgasbord."

Henry's finely crafted prose can bring a scene to life in vivid detail. The chapter titled "Long Awaited Rain in an Ohio Woods" is a descriptive masterpiece. He can make a description fairly sparkle:

"The white flowers of this orchid are arranged in a double spiral on a spike, resembling a Fourth-of-July sparkler with white sparks flying from the slender rod." And the word-pictures are enhanced by a good collection of photos.

Each chapter is, in effect, a lesson in how to find new knowledge and delightful pastime by becoming aware of the wonder in the commonplace. Here is a clear alternative to the contrived, artificial entertainment of the electronic media.

A brief scripture text sets the tone for each nature essay. A general theme for the entire collection might be Genesis 1:31: "And God saw everything that he had made, and behold, it was very good."

Open this book anywhere and you will find delight, insight and inspiration while gaining a fuller appreciation of the natural world. The author's underlying message also comes through: Respect and preserve the Earth and its creatures, thereby serving humanity and honoring the Creator.

—Robert M. Schrag
Editor, *Mennonite Weekly Review*
Newton, Kansas

Table of Contents

Part I

Winter

February sunset at Basinger Woods, Bluffton, Ohio

Winter Woods Offer Lively Panorama

Thou hast made the moon to mark the seasons;
the sun knows its time of setting.
Thou makest darkness, and it is night,
when all the beasts of the forest creep forth.
— Psalm 104:19-20

A woods in winter presents a very different aspect than it does in spring and summer.

It seems strange how the trail that loops parallel to the one you are treading often appears so close in winter. During the summer, hidden by vegetation in between, it could seem to be far away and therefore maybe more mysterious.

Individual trees along the way also appear more personal and more worthy of closer attention in winter. We notice and appreciate the bark of the white ash for the pleasing netted or diamond pattern so characteristic of the species.

The tightly-wrapped bark of the American beech is gray, smooth, neat—beautiful in its simplicity. Sometimes it has a remnant of coppery-toned foliage that shimmers crisply during a slight breeze, adding to its subdued magic.

—March 11, 1993

•

Early one evening when I approached Marty and Minnie Miller Basinger's Woods near

Bluffton, Ohio, I saw the characteristic emphatic flit of wings that projected a dark-backed prairie horned lark at a level flight a few feet above the open field. Later, its song of tiny fairy-like bells came floating over the mottled ground that was slowly thawing under a February sun.

This colorful bird reminds me of a miniature meadowlark. It is an early nester. Like the sower of spring oats in Kansas, it often begins its operations while late winter winds send drifts of delicate crystals hurrying through the fields. It is normal for a horned lark on incubation duties to be covered with a March snow or two. These "road trotters" must get an early start at rearing young, for here in Ohio, at least, three broods may be raised in a year.

One February I watched several horned larks ascend high in the sky over a prairie. Like the skylark of Europe, the horned lark sings as it performs its aerial flight.

•

Along the west edge of the Basinger Woods, the scrubbed-down look of the beech trees made them conspicuous against the background of darker trees and shrubs at the north end of the plot. Their crisp leaves rattled dryly in the wind.

Clawing through the grainy snow at the base of a large oak, I sought last autumn's leaves and acorn cups to help identify the species. I found a weathered chalice with fragments of moss-like fringes on its edge, along with a few leaves bearing top-heavy blades–both clues indicating the tree to be the mossy-cup or burr oak.

Sandwiched between two oak leaves was the cocoon of a moth that kept its identity hidden from this intruder unfamiliar with its particular style of winterwear. The firmness of the pupa indicated that it was alive and well, but, if so, it was fortunate not to have been discovered by an animal prowler snuffling through the duff in search of just such a juicy tidbit. I temporarily tucked the cocoon into my pocket, hoping that, come next spring, the occupant of the cocoon would step forth and declare its identity.

•

As I continued southward, a family group of slender ironwood came into view. These modest understory stalwarts are often overlooked in the midst of overtowering hard woods.

Because of their smooth, rippling trunks, they have gained the descriptive name of musclewood. Along the rounded ridges and in the hollows of their sinewy trunks are narrow bands and other patterns in various colors, all of which contributes a certain fascinating quality to this friendly woods.

The clucks of migrating blackbirds flying in loose formations drew my attention to feathery, wispy clouds forming high in the dulling blue sky.

A partially decomposed log, lying among the litter, exposed an open side cluttered with remains of acorn and hickory nut shells–a reminder of shy four-footed beasties inhabiting the woodland. By leaving their kitchen middens in plain view, they announce the reality of their presence and their right to be there as citizens of the woodland community.

•

As the sun sank lower, a small, dark form moved near a clump of snow-stiffened grass. Then it disappeared.

High in a tree, a white-breasted nuthatch, talking to itself or maybe hinting its position to others of its clan, ceased its twangy musing and disappeared in the growing darkness.

Finally, a late-winter sunset traced a shimmering trail of light diffused by the clump of lindens behind which it was slowing slipping, seeming to hang there momentarily. The domed domicile of a fox squirrel swayed in the top of a hickory. A redtailed-hawk sailed in from the southwest and settled among the oaks, lindens, and beeches.

Night was coming on. A whole new set of dramas would replace those more usually witnessed by woods watchers who visit the Basinger woodland community from time to time.

—March 11, 1982

Sounds of a Winter Woods

The wind blows where it wills, and you hear the sound of it, but you do not know whence it comes or whither it goes...
            —John 3:8

The sounds of a winter woods are as varied as the moods of each passing day and hour.

One winter afternoon in Luke and Dorothy Bauman Luginbihl's woods near Bluffton, I heard sounds unique to each part of the woods as I hiked along the trail from one area to another. They were sounds that changed as the hours and even the minutes moved ahead.

A winter woods

At the north end, the wind was rather muted at first. Later a dull whistling emanated from the tops of the mostly leafless trees.

Soon the sharp chip of a downy woodpecker called attention to the area nearby. That call was quickly followed by a deadened pecking pattern like a tiny hammer beating a bounding tattoo on a branch of punky wood. Soon the bird's dipping flight took it high into a tree at the east border of the plot. With a sidling motion it maneuvered to one side of the trunk, seeming to make sure to keep the observer under surveillance. Then its lilting flight took it out of sight. Again I became a listener aware of the utterings of a winter woods.

In the distance, a faint whimper of wings indicated a single mourning dove taking flight. Farther along in the woods and closer to me, I observed a quintet of doves burst forth with loud flappings followed a few moments later by a trio, then a pair–some circled to the southeast, while others headed back into the middle of the woods.

The muffled noise of the wind at the south end of the tract was now north of me. I had passed the larger trees and was in the midst of low shrubbery less affected by the wind in the treetops.

Over the bare field now south, a strong southwest wind was driving the snow at a sharp angle.

Turning back northward I saw more startled doves as they took to the chilly air, the sharp whine of their wings contrasting with the sullen, blustering wind pounding its way through the tops of the tall hickory, maple, and beech.

•

A sudden creak and a hoarse groan broke from a large hop hornbeam that had just been struck by a strong blast of insistent wind. I needed little imagination to feel that the tree was in pain and was protesting as it strained to maintain its proud posture. But the bullying southwester continued to push and shove its way around the resisting trunks and limbs of the woodland establishment.

•

Under a huge beech at the north end, I had finally come full circle. But now the sound from the other end of the wood was reminiscent of the roar of a waterfall or the rumble of a train. Something ominous in its tone was being transferred to this area where, earlier, I had heard only a subdued whistling.

Fluttering of unshed maple leaves joined with a dry, rasping clatter of papery offerings still clinging to the old beech, to add a new section in an orchestration that seemed to be building up to a dramatic crescendo.

Even wilder were the jagged, discordant sounds contributed as background music by two towering spruce trees a stone's throw to the northeast on the Clarence Jone's farm. There the gale seemed as if it were desperately attempting to wrench the tops from the veterans that had for years successfully resisted the onslaughts of raging winds and crushing snows.

Rather reluctantly I trudged out of the plot, strangely moved by the intimate, soothing whisperings as well as by the discordant, ominous, and defiant utterances of a winter woods.

—January 8, 1981

Winter Birds at Feeders

Look at the birds of the air: they neither sow nor reap...
and yet your heavenly Father feeds them.
—Matthew 6:26

On a bone-chilling winter morning at our home in Bluffton, Ohio, I put on my warmest coat and went outside to fill the bird

feeders. A fluffed-up but perky black-capped chickadee was hurriedly selecting large black-and-white sunflower seeds from our

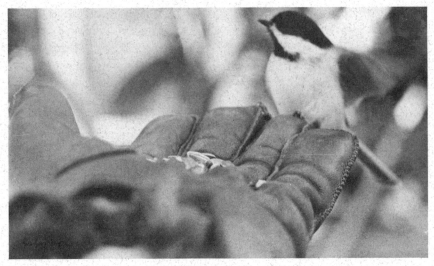

A bird in the hand . . .

terraced patio. Then, without as much as a fare-thee-well, he dashed off to secret them under the bark of a tree, quickly returned for another load, and darted away again without a backward glance. Apparently he was determined to hide as many seeds as possible before the supply was gone.

Noting that the little fellow seemed to have no fear of me, I decided to see if he would eat from my hand. First I went inside and put on my furred gloves for protection from the bitter cold. Back outside I poured a fistful of seeds into my gloved left hand and clasped the camera under my chin. I was hoping that the bird would be lured into taking a seed from my gloved hand and I could take its photo. I hardly had time to focus the camera before the little fellow lit on my glove, picked up a seed, and was up and away at the click of the camera shutter.

I tried that maneuver several times, but because the air was so solidly cold, I soon dashed back into the warmth of the house, feeling pleased with the excitement of hand-feeding the black-capped tit.

•

Another chickadee happening took place when we lived in Wadsworth, Ohio.

That winter was marked with heavy snows and cold temperatures. For the wintering birds, I placed a board as a feeding platform on a south-facing windowsill. Noticing a number of chickadees and other wintering birds shopping at the feeder, I took a handful of sunflower seeds and went out to scatter them on the feeding platform.

One chickadee picked up a seed, but instead of flying away with it as the others had done, he remained on the platform. Out of curiosity, I held out my hand. The bird, trying to do me a favor, I suppose, dropped the seed he had in his beak and picked another one from my hand.

My cashmere coat was brushed up against the feeder; the chickadee flitted to the coat and clung there as it dashed the seed against the edge of the board as though trying to shell it. I was amazed at this action, for the bird behaved as though it had absolutely no fear of me and was pleased to demonstrate the fact by its trusting behavior.

−January 28, 1993

•

One day my wife, Glennys, and I visited Betty Bixel Heiks, who lives on the woody banks of Big Riley Creek near Bluffton. At Betty's home we watched as a diverse gathering of winter birds fed on seed she had sprinkled generously on the deck that wrapped around the south and east sides of the house.

Downy woodpeckers, dapper and confident in their black-and-white carpenter outfits, whittled away almost continuously at the chunks of suet that hung on railing posts along the deck.

Suddenly Betty called our attention to a red-bellied woodpecker that had paused warily at a suet station. Perhaps deeming the little downies mere pipsqueaks among the woodworking fraternity, the rather classy woodpecker quickly flew off to await another time for supping at the suet free from the presence of its bold cousins.

Then a pair of black-capped chickadees came hustling in as if they had not a moment to spare. Not even bidding us the time of day, each chickadee snatched a sunflower seed and dove out of sight. Their sudden entrance and exit left us with but a blurred memory of the sleek forms of those in-a-hurry feathered dandies who briefly enlivened the scene of a cold winter woods along Riley Creek.

•

Pert and bright-eyed, a tufted titmouse, its gray, peaked stocking cap tilted at a jaunty "I'm-really-something" angle, followed the efficient procedure of its chickadee cousins. It hastily picked something from the deck and without further adieu, did hie itself away, probably to quickly hide its bit of food in some cranny of bark or fissure of splintered branch for future use.

•

A handsome male cardinal landed confidently on the deck where its scarlet finery was accented sharply against the back-drop of snow and darkened tree trunks.

Using thin branches as a swaying highway over which to travel toward the platform, a slender red squirrel floated to the deck with ballet-dancer lightness. There it deftly garnered some seeds, then swiftly moved over twigs and branches and disappeared from sight.

With even more aplomb than the self-assured redbird, a blue jay plopped itself down for a fill-up of sunflower fruits. Methodically picking up three or four seeds which it stored in its throat-pouch, the blue jay jostled the seeds about as it tried to add several others to its payload.

When a fellow jaybird hit the deck, the first bird took off, no doubt for a storing session in the woods nearby. No matter how carefully and secretly the wily jay cached its emergency rations, nuthatches, chickadees, titmice, and their kin would also share in the goodies the jay stored in its sundry hiding places near Betty's home along Big Riley Creek.

—February 25, 1988

An Ice Concert and a Jamboree

From whose womb did the ice come forth,
and who has given birth to the hoarfrost of heaven?
The waters become hard like stone,
and the face of the deep is frozen.
—Job 38:29-30

For a moment, one frigid morning when I started out walking the quarry, I thought the humming sound in the air was that of tires–semi-trucks speeding along the highway less than a mile away. Then a musical, plucked-string *boing* burst forth from the quarry. There followed a series of bright, taut-string notes, zinging lightly over the ice and disappearing into the beyond. I was delighted. I knew it was the February ice–singing again!

After that tantalizing introduction, I slowly followed the quarry, pausing as the ice music chimed forth again and again. Many were the crystal renditions that morning as the various layers of thin ice sheets and the solid ice blanket were whipped into contortions and ripplings by a relentless southwest wind.

After having come half-circle around the quarry, I stopped to scatter duck feed at the northeast corner. Suddenly I was startled by

Big Riley Creek nearing spring breakup

a sharp explosion that cracked and echoed in the solid, frigid air like the report of a giant whip. Apparently the thick armor of ice had split under the blast of the wind, heaving and swelling the icy waters that could no longer be restrained.

Retracing my steps, I heard the siren songs trip brightly along the way, tinkling, vibrating, like crystals splintering, tempting this heavy-footed mortal to tear away from the less intoxicating offerings of the day. Not often do I hear the ice music. Why didn't I stay? Will the ice sing again tomorrow...ever?

•

Several days earlier, with my pocketknife I had pruned the purple twigs of the box elder along the quarry path. Then one morning, a two-inch icicle hung stiffly from one of the severed branches. Snapping it off, I tasted the icy offering. Sure enough, a faint but definitely sweet flavor put me on notice that though the sweetness was slight, it was strong enough to be sensed by taste.

The box elder tree is one of the *Acers*, the maples. Native Americans used this tree as well as other maple species for processing sugar, though the sap does not compare with the sugar maple in both quantity and content.

Perhaps the little red squirrel that my friend Darwin Luginbuhl watched years ago as it nibbled an icicle just may have plucked it from a broken maple twig. But sweetened or not, there's no reason why a reasonable little red Jimmy shouldn't like to chew on ice just as we do.

—February 25, 1993

•

Witnessing an ice jamboree on Big Riley Creek can be a jarring experience for the observer as well as for the raging stream.

High drama was taking place that day just east of the swinging bridge near the college cabin at the Bluffton College Nature Preserve. After a sudden meltdown, great chunks of ice came crushing down on the still unbroken ice sheet to the west.

A crunching, grinding din arose as the huge masses heaved against the layer ahead. Immense blocks ground upward and slid onto the solid crust. Other giant crystalline monsters brazenly shouldered their way forward, forming a jagged ice barricade against the onslaught of the raging flood tearing down the creek from the east.

With a sudden discordant crash, the ice sheet finally broke up just west of the swinging bridge. Behind the ice jam, the swirling waters of mud and dirty foam quickly rose a foot or so higher.

Meanwhile, the terrific pressure of the blockaded flood forced the mass to grind and gouge away at the creek banks, crunching and chewing small trees and shrubs, wrenching branches from helpless trees bordering the flood.

The restrained flood waters dashed and bullied at the planks of the bridge, threatening to destroy the structure. Suddenly the drift gave way with a cacophony of crunchings, crashings, and groans.

Finally, the waters leveled off, flowing angrily to the west. There, no doubt, other confrontations between ice and flood continued to erupt in unrelenting combat.

•

Crystalline ice mixed among dried leaves and wood chips, brittle and eggshell-like, crunched under our feet as we walked the winter woods at the Bluffton College Nature Preserve. With me was Galen Burkholder, a visitor from Pennsylvania, whose family enjoys camping and the out-of-doors.

As Galen and I moved slowly along the trail above the pond, a sedate flock of more than 20 score of huge Canada Geese mulled about on the ice. Once in a while a few of the flat-foots squawked out a raucous announcement to liven the crowd a bit.

All the while, they seemed to be enjoying their rest stop even though they stood on the ice, without galoshes of any kind, as barefoot as a tender gosling just out of its warm eggshell. How they manage to keep their feet cozy is a mystery they may understand, although we stand in awe of their tough standing-gears.

−March 11, 1993

Doves Winter in Midwest Cornfields

Look at the birds of the air; they neither sow nor reap
...and yet your heavenly Father feeds them.
                                    −Matthew 6:26

Hundreds of doves winter here in Ohio where waste grain is usually abundant in the corn fields.

One December day I watched an individual in a small flock sitting in the snow on the patio. The hungry dove was greedily cramming corn down its gullet. No doubt it had taken some kernels before my count began, but it swallowed at least 23 grains as I watched.

Taking no chances on being caught short when the weather was threatening and the supply ample, the bird resorted to drastic tactics. With wings akimbo and neck outstretched to increase its capacity, the dove shivered and shook like an old-fashioned fanning mill. A last final attempt resulted in a kernel toppling out of its beak and into the snow.

Like an overloaded transport plane, the dove finally took off, barely clearing the fence as it headed for a tree. Here was at least one dove that was prudent, though maybe a bit eccentric. It probably survived the severe winter−perhaps because it knew how to jostle and shake while other more decorous individuals might refuse to condescend to such crude behavior, especially in the presence of others.

•

In the Southwest, not only mourning doves but the white-winged, Inca, and ground doves are found in various areas.

In the Tucson Valley of Arizona, the Christmas Bird Count of 1976 netted a total of 1,684 Inca doves and 31 ringed turtle-doves. White-winged doves totaled 17, while 773 mourning doves were observed.

The Christmas Bird Count at Phoenix tallied 89 ground doves and 829 Incas. I remember when Bethel College professor Dwight

Platt of Newton, Kansas, and I saw our first white-winged doves in Texas at Big Bend National Park and on the Edwards Plateau. White-winged doves are beautiful creatures and are easy to identify.

•

Residents of the Los Angeles area become acquainted with two exotics: the ringed turtle-dove and the spotted dove. My brother Ralph of Montrose, introduced me to the two species while I was visiting him. Even as far east as Wichita, Kansas, the 1976 Christmas Bird Count netted two Incas, and in 1975 two ringed turtle-doves were observed.

So while we enjoy mourning doves out this way, people in the Southwest enjoy other species as well.

•

Mourning doves are rather successful breeders in spite of the high mortality rates of their eggs and young.

One late winter day, March 3, I saw a dove toting nesting material to the blue spruces in the yard of our next door neighbors, Herbert and Kathleen Kindle. Now that's an early start—nearly as good as the great horned owl and horned lark.

At Marion County Lake near Marion, Kansas, I once found a nest with two eggs being actively incubated in October. It is doubtful that the attempt was successful at that time of the year, but it does show that the mourning dove is no slacker when it comes to providing for perpetuation of its own kind.

—November 24, 1977

Bluffton College Nature Preserve

Great are the works of the Lord,
studied by all who have pleasure in them.
            —Psalm 111:2

Mother Nature, along with the help of her sunshine and wind, can change the shape of a sawtooth sunflower leaf from lanceolate to corkscrew—both pleasing designs.

One autumn when I was walking through the strip of prairie that the college botanist, Maurice Kauffman, had planted on the Bluffton College Nature Preserve, I came upon a sawtooth sunflower plant, *Helianthus grosseserratus*. Some of its leaves were still green; others had dried and seared. The process of desiccation had slowly drawn the leaves into a corkscrew design.

The unusual coil pattern caught my attention. I was surprised and intrigued to discover that the motif was not just a chance occurrence, but that many of the dried leaves took the form of a corkscrew, a seemingly unusual design in nature.

The sawtooth sunflower flourishes in certain prairies in Ohio. I had transplanted some from a roadside ditch near Bowling Green, Ohio. Now established in our garden, their bright golden blossoms are much appreciated in late summer.

—January 28, 1988

•

On the day after Christmas, I walked the trail in the South Woods of the Bluffton College Nature Preserve with our pastor Mel Schmidt, his daughter Kim Schmidt, and her husband David Navari. It was a bitterly cold morning. Ice crystals crunched beneath our feet as we tromped the shadowy path, which was covered with various shades of brown, crisp leaves.

The vegetation along the trail was sear and stark, the trees, rigidly still and stiffly erect. The frigid, 20-degree air packed itself around each participant in the wintery scene. Our attention centered mostly on the assorted de-

Nature's designs: even the corkscrew motif

signs and textures of bark wrapped around each tree species.

Most of the black cherry trees, *Prunus serotina*, were clothed in varied patterns of peeling bark, red-edged and curled, although some still retained smooth, gray, wraparound garments that could be easily mistaken for bark of some other species. Perhaps the trees were masking their identity because they are sometimes rustled for their valuable wood, possibly second only to black walnut on our lumber market.

We also ran our hands over the rippling bark of the American hornbean, *Carpinus caroliniana*. Its sinewy trunk beneath the smooth bark has given it the name of musclewood.

Nearby were eastern hop hornbeam, or ironwood, *Ostrya*

virginiana. Even though the leaves of the two hornbeams are very similar, the bark is quite different. The eastern hop hornbeam is shreddy and broken into thick, narrow scales. The wood is heavy and hard, fully deserving the name, ironwood.

—January 28, 1993

•

Rudely disturbed by some inquisitive hikers, the snow-white larva, photographed here, was revealed where it lay rocked in a cradle of a hackberry leaf.

If left to itself, this tiny insect would probably have spun itself a cozy sleeping bag and changed into a tough pupa. With the coming of warmer weather, it would have developed into a tiny, expert leaf roller or leaf folder and gone on its merry way.

Near the larva you may see the tiny tower-like protuberance

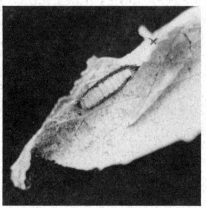

Larva wrapped in leaf tip

formed by a hackberry nipple-gall insect that also uses the hackberry leaf to form a shelter and nursery for these minute creatures as they develop. Evidently the galls do not cause much harm to the hackberry tree, for sometimes hundreds of the little rounded huts are found on a single tree.

—February 25, 1988

Exploring Nature Preserve With Children

The earth is the Lord's and the fulness thereof,
the world and those who dwell therein...
—Psalm 24:1

When my daughter, Carol Drake, and her children spent several hours with me at the Bluffton College Nature Preserve one December day, we enjoyed many aspects of the area. One of the interesting experiences we had was seeing praying mantid egg masses, noting their unique design.

A mantid egg mass on a multiflora rose bush, as this one was, would seem secure among the many thorns. But, in spite of the eggs being in a relatively safe position amongst the briars, enterprising predators always seem to find ways to penetrate such defenses.

Many of the dozens of egg masses we found that December day had been pecked open by the little downy woodpecker, something I had seen a number of times in my years of bird watching.

One might presume that these tiny eggs, though numerous inside the dried frothy mass, would hardly fill the chisel-beak of the small woodpecker. Yet a goodly number of the plundered egg masses taken together probably provide a sufficient snack during the little carpenter's work day.

•

Benjamin, who was six years old then, and his brother and sister, nine-year-old Christian and eight-year-old Julia, were especially delighted to locate and examine the many deserted bird nests that were now revealed after leaf-fall. They found tufts of cattail cotton in most of the nests. Some of this material was used to bind the nests together. It also provided cushiony linings for the comfort of nestlings snugly huddled inside the nests.

Mantid egg mass in multiflora rose bush

I can still hear Ben cry out to Carol, "Mom! I found a *beautiful* one!" Christian's delight was to climb the trees for a close-up look at the nests, especially the larger ones.

Julia and I trudged toward the south end of the pond where its soggy border was lined with a strip of cattails. We were searching for abandoned red-winged blackbird nests. The major part of the nests were made of cattail material, but since many of the plants were broken and bending over the cattail debris, it was no small task for my granddaughter and me to locate the nests.

Nonetheless, we did find several, and we examined the way the red-wing had used the broad leaves to weave and bind the nest to the stems of surrounding cattails. We could well imagine the "o-ka-lees" of last summer's males' territorial call accompanied by their flashing red-and-yellow shoulder pads which warned others of their tribe to refrain from trespassing on their well-marked claims. This day, however, was a quiet and peaceful one. We will have to wait until late February and early March to again see and hear the males as they stake out their territories. However, we sometimes have a few males visit our feeders in early winter. Our few sightings have been in January.

•

Down along the floodplain, we watched a little red squirrel as it madly streaked through the tree tops. The nasal "squanks" of a white-breasted nuthatch announced the presence of the little upside-down bird as it searched creviced bark for some morsel to sustain its energy. In the distance a crow announced its business route, while a blue jay cared not a whit if its brash call disturbed the peace.

After an hour-and-a-half or more, our daughter, the children, and I returned to Bluffton. Ours had been a rewarding and exciting time of exploring at the preserve.

—January 9, 1992

•

While visiting Carol and her family at their home in Manchester, Massachusetts, I found that wildlife was plentiful in the urban area where they live.

A rather light-colored opossum came up to the yard regularly at night to seek tidbits just within range of the yard light. It eagerly munched on some sunflower seeds left ungleaned by white-breasted nuthatches, black-capped chickadees, tufted titmice and squirrels.

Later a black skunk appeared on the lawn, undaunted by human inhabitants of the vicinity.

•

Daytime brought fluffy gray squirrels to the area. They kept very busy rustling through the dry leaves and, later, frequenting the feeders we had hung at several locations close to the house. They appeared lighter in color than the gray squirrels we see in Bluffton.

One of the squirrels found little two-year-old Benjamin no threat as the bushytail scrounged around on one side of the glass door while the bright-eyed boy was fascinated by the closeness of the squirrel just on the other side of the glass.

We heard crows in the area almost constantly. We also saw some perched in the pines just outside the yard. One day, Carol saw a huge, crow-sized pileated woodpecker in the area, its red crest flashing in the winter sunshine.

•

Christian and Julia, who were six and four years old at the time, and I prepared and hung suet bags close to the house at various places. A female downy woodpecker soon located one near the swing, while a male with a small red patch in the back of the head, frequented another bag on the other side of the house. I never saw either downy in the other bird's territory.

Anyway, the wildlife was busy those December days near the Drake home at the top of a hill in suburban Manchester.

—January 28, 1988

Now Memories Are All That Remain

A voice was heard in Ramah,
wailing and loud lamentation,
Rachel weeping for her children;
she refused to be consoled,
because they were no more.
    —Matthew 2:18

When our daughter, Carol Drake, and her children were visiting us over the holidays, we took a stroll over to the National Quarry to my duck feeding station.

A few days earlier, I had a very unique experience as I fed the flock of about 20 wild mallards that were regulars at the feeding station. I was hoping for a repeat performance when the children—Julia, Christian, and Benjamin—tossed corn out onto the ice. And soon the quackers came winging in from an open area of water toward the middle of the quarry.

The ice near shoreline was thin and must have had a fine film of moisture on the surface. As the ducks attempted to land, their outstretched orange landing gear hit the icy surface. When they back-flapped their wings and used their tails as rudders to help slow their forward motion the ducks executed perfect three-point landings and rather gracefully skidded a little ways on the ice. Marvelous!

The ice was so slippery that in order to gobble up each grain of corn, the ducks refrained from spinning their wheels, and instead they scooted about on their tummies in a rather ludicrous manner. Although their efforts were amusing to Benjamin, Julia, and

Christian, as well as to Carol and me, the flatfoots must have considered it serious business. No doubt it was just that. —*From Wayside Revelations, January 23, 1992.*

•

Flocks of herring gulls were gathered on the grounds of the famous Arnold Arboretum near Boston on a winter day. Several outspoken crows scrounged around the area, intently gathering scraps left by arboretum visitors.

I had been delighted when our daughter, Carol, suggested a visit to the Arnold Arboretum. I had been hoping to have an opportunity to explore a New England winter woods, which is as fascinating in its own way as such a woods in any other season.

Carol, David, and I kept busy renewing acquaintances with trees that were old friends, and getting to know and recognize trees new to us. The children—Christian,7, Julia, 5, and 3-year-old Ben—ran down wooded hillsides, stopping to handle snow along the trails and discovering many interesting things to investigate.

Three or four hours quickly passed before we left Arnold Arboretum. All agreed that our enjoyment as a family tramping in a winter woods was very satisfying. —*From Wayside Revelations, March 23, 1989.*

•

MWR—Editor's Note: *Carol Henry Drake died November 29, 1993, at age 45, after suffering an aneurysm three days earlier. She was visiting her parents Roy and Glennys Kaufman Henry in Bluffton, Ohio, for the holidays.*

Carol lived in Florence, Massachusetts, and was studying horticulture and landscape design at the Stockbridge School of the University of Massachusetts. She had volunteered as a parent aide at Children's Aid & Family Services in Northhampton, Massachusettes and had been a volunteer and room mother at Leeds Elementary School, where her children were enrolled.

Besides her parents, survivors include her husband, David; two sons, Christian and Benjamin, both at home; a daughter, Julia, at home; a brother, Lyle Henry of Bluffton; and a sister, Mona Henry of Columbus, Ohio. A brother, Larry Henry, died in 1990.

—*January 6, 1994*

California sea lions sun themselves on the rocky shore of Monterey Bay

Sea Lions Rule Rocky Domains

Be glad, earth and sky!
Roar, sea, and every creature in you....
  —Psalm 96:11 (Good News Bible)

The large bull California sea lion, from his preeminent position on the rock, holds most of his audience in rapt attention like a dignified headmaster commanding the respect of his pupils.

While in the water together, pups have the protection of the bulls who also patrol the waters next to their rookeries where they maintain loosely knit harems. The bulls also make threatening gestures toward any male who may appear to harbor intentions of invading their domain.

And here on the breakwater in Monterey Bay, the imposing-looking bull in the photo seems to have solid control over the cows, as well as the older pups in the group around him.

•

While camping at Veterans Park in Monterey this January, I could hear the honking bark of the sea lions whenever I was awake late at night, even though they were over a mile away in the bay at Fishermen's Wharf. Fishing boats came and went throughout the night; some fishermen cleaned their fish on the dock and perhaps threw scraps to the ever-hungry sea lions, who barked for more.

During daylight and evening hours, concessionaires sell fish portions to visitors who are entertained by the antics of the sea lions yelping in raucous monotony as they dive for the handouts, sometimes snatching a treat before it strikes the water. Evidently a number of the sleek sea mammals depend, in part at least, on seafood thrown to them by fishermen and visitors.

•

The California sea lion is the trained seal of circuses, parks, and marine shows. Even in the wild, this sea lion reportedly engages in antics, tossing objects and catching them on its nose. Extremely intelligent, it is able to learn rapidly. Its memory is keen, for even after several months of not practicing its act, it can perform again almost perfectly.

The one species contains three populations in as many distinct geographical areas: the western coast of North America from Mexico to Vancouver Island, the Galapagos Islands, and the Sea of Japan. The latter population is sometimes considered extinct, even though reports persist of its existence on Dakto Island.

—March 26, 1987

Whales Enjoy Breaching, Skyhopping

There is the sea, vast and spacious,
Teeming with creatures beyond number—
Living things both large and small.
There the ships go to and fro,
And the Leviathan, which you formed to frolic there.
These all look to you
To give them their food at the proper time.
—Psalm 104:25-27 (New International Version)

In the photograph on the next page, the two objects projecting just above the water on each side of the diving whale's tail indicate that there may have been two other whales nearby for the breeding season. Besides the mating pair of gray whales, there is often a third whale, a male consort, that accompanies the court

Gray whale starting on a deep dive

ing couple. The projections may be flippers, for the gray whale has no topside or dorsal fin.

Some whale watchers say that when the whale, *Eschrichtius robustus,* lifts its tail high above the water in this position, it is just commencing a deep dive, for in shallow dives it does not brandish its tail in this manner.

Another interesting behavior trait of the gray whale is "breaching," or leaping partly out of the water, often falling back with a great splash. "Skyhopping" is the lifting of the head vertically out of the water, as the whale apparently looks around. Both forms of behavior seem to be common during migration and at calving and mating grounds. We saw skyhopping from our boat on a number of occasions. Various explanations for the two habits have been suggested. Among them is the thought that perhaps it is just "fun."

•

During their southward migration, the gray whales pass close to shore. From the elevation at the Point Reyes lighthouse, we saw several gray whales, even in the surf not far from the beach. The site was thronged with eager watchers hoping for sight of the graybacks; many of them were rewarded with sightings.

Gray whales are perhaps the best known whales to many people because they come in close to the shore and can also be approached closely in small boats.

At times this species seems

not only to tolerate people but indeed appears to solicit their attention. In the San Ignacio Lagoon along the outer coast of Baja, visitors have touched, rubbed, and even scratched the backs of the great sea monsters.

Several years ago in Massachusetts Bay, our small boat was approached so closely by a humpback whale that the animal was only a few feet from us, seemingly curious about the excited creatures on board. We were fascinated by its friendly manner. The Pacific humpback whales, *Megaptera novaeangliae*, once numbering in the thousands, were almost extirpated from the Pacific. With protection, there are now about 300, and the population is slowly growing. Some are seen along the California coast during migration.

•

On an all-day boat trip, we were fortunate to sight a number of Risso's dolphins, *Grampus griseus*, or grampus. At times they were close to the front of the boat near the surface of the water.

A grampus has a large topside or dorsal fin. It is a large dolphin, about 13 feet long. Not having the beaked snout of most other dolphins, the grampus head rises almost straight up from the upper jaw.

Pelorus Jack, a dolphin who was given lifelong protection by the government of New Zealand, is thought to have been a grampus. Pelorus Jack was known for his frolicking around ships. He endeared himself to sailors who thought he guided them into Pelorus Sound. The famous dolphin was observed from 1896 to 1916. He was over 20 years old when he died.

Risso's dolphin seems to enjoy riding the bow waves of ships and leaping from the water in apparent abandon. Perhaps, like the whale with its skyhopping and breaching, the dolphin is just having a lot of fun.

—April 9, 1987

Brave, Clever Squirrels Find Free Food

Bless the Lord, all his works, in all places of his dominion.
Bless the Lord, O my soul!

–Psalm 103:22

Our California ground squirrel appears to be enjoying a tidbit found on the beach near San Simeon. Perhaps, however, that rather cold January day when I saw few visitors along that stretch of coast, there were fewer shared snacks for such beasties, gulls, crows, and the like.

As I stopped to check on what manner of wildlife might be up and about, I photographed a few business-like crows, heard various gulls, but at first spotted no ground squirrels.

Then I sat on a boulder a short distance from the line of salt water foam, and I glimpsed a dark movement a few rods away. Finally a California ground squirrel appeared.

I had scattered a bit of gorp (a mixture of soy beans, peanuts, and other seeds) on the sandy beach where a loose flock of Brewer's blackbirds was hanging around to take advantage of anything they could feed on. Soon the ground squirrel approached and found something to suit its fancy.

Then, as though a message had been quickly sent–mysteriously, marvelously–several of its

Slim pickings for a California ground squirrel on a beach in January

kin appeared, then a few more. Finally a nice gang of about a dozen had gathered round, busily but daintily nibbling on the seeds and nuts spread out on the sandy table.

Then I became curious to find out if they would dare to share the large boulder on which I sat. When the only morsels left were beside me on the boulder, a few of the bolder ones climbed up and were soon mincing away beside me in a rather cozy fashion.

Finally I became inquisitive enough to venture another experiment. Leaving the boulder, I found a smooth area on the beach. There I lay down and stretched out and then placed an unhulled double peanut between my teeth.

The squirrels had followed me to my new location and perhaps were a bit puzzled by my actions, especially when they had spied the huge peanut I was holding in my mouth. Finally, one approached rather close to me, then hesitated, and eventually backed off as though considering such an action a bit too cheeky even for a bright-eyed *Citellus beecheyi.*

At last, however, a bold individual cautiously approached. Stretching forward a bit, it carefully and delicately seized the peanut with its teeth and removed it.

The daring one then moved a few yards away and nonchalantly removed the shell and nibbled the kernels as though the whole operation was all in a day's work. And perhaps it was.

Although for me the venture was a delightful one, I'll admit that when the ground squirrel and I were nose-to-nose and eyeball-to-eyeball, I had a strange feeling for a moment or two.

Oh well! Nothing ventured, nothing gained. And if the nervy little mammal could have talked, it may have expressed the same sentiment.

—January 23, 1992

•

Eastern gray squirrel with his own windbreak

Though the winter wind comes storming in from the southwest, and the snow sweeps along with the bitter blasts, our town-bred gray squirrels somehow manage to come out most days for their daily bread.

The bushytail pictured here is not only partly shielded by the trunk of our apple tree, but its full, wide tail also helps protect it from our northwestern Ohio winds.

The squirrels get rather sociable at this time of the year, sometimes peeking through the south window of the study, often not moving even when I stand close to the window. Only if Ashley Ashford the Third, our big blue cat, lunges against the pane, will they leap for the cedar tree from which they will return in due time. They hardly give a wink as Ashes-the-Cat takes a catnap just below the window. They know the cat's limitations and take full advantage of eating beyond the reach of the feline twitching his tail in frustration in full sight of his tantalizing quarry just beyond the window.

•

A gray squirrel finally found how to get sunflower seeds that had hitherto been reserved for titmice, nuthatches, and chickadees. The seeds were inside a length of hollow log suspended by wire from the grape arbor out of reach, I thought, of the crafty squirrels.

One day I noticed a squirrel dangling from the log by its hind legs, its front paws holding a sunflower seed. Although upside down, the clever bushy-tail was contentedly munching on the kernel he had managed to coax out of the crevice. There he hung quite a while until he had his fill of the goodies. Now it was up to me to try to devise a contraption that I could use to thwart the wily gray squirrels from monopolizing the sunflower feeder.

•

A gray squirrel and a cottontail may not seem to have much in common. Yet, these two different mammals were seen hobnobbing together one morning at the south end of Bluffton.

Perhaps the squirrel wondered why the cottontail had a short tail and long ears, while the rabbit was perplexed by its companion's long tail and short ears. Maybe they were even comparing notes, pondering why one nibbled grass and tender herbs, while the other preferred acorns and nuts.

One thing these city-living dudes had in common, however: both liked handouts of corn, especially in winter when it was sometimes hard to come by. But in this respect, such offerings were placed high on shelves where the cottontail could only glean what leftovers fell to the ground from the squirrel's table.

•

When I was visiting Oris and Ginny O'Neal, Rittman, Ohio, a photo of a gray squirrel brought out this story: The O'Neals were visiting at the home of friends when a scratching sound was heard at the door. The host and hostess seemed not in the least surprised when they opened the door and in bounded a squirrel who seemed familiar with the house and household.

It was a squirrel they had befriended since it had been quite young. Evidently the crafty squirrel knew where he could get what he needed to hold body and soul together in spite of spiraling inflation. It was free from the uncertainty of changes in government entitlement programs and would get along as a bona-fide member of the provident household.

•

A snowplow the red squirrel is not!

One winter day when a thick layer of powdery snow covered the land, a little red jimmy was seen desperately lunging his way along toward a tree. Its frenzied dashes gained it little headway, as it sank in the loose crystal stuff where even its head momentarily disappeared from sight. A slight pause taken to get its breath brought the powdery snow caving down on the poor squirrel.

When he finally reached the safety of a tree, the squirrel was exhausted. This time it did not scamper merrily up the trunk as the vivacious beastie is wont to do; it just hung there, its tail drooped–miserable, bedraggled and limp, not the brandishing standard of a saucy red jimmy. If its tail quivered, it was not that of a self-assured, scolding red squirrel, for the only chattering it did was from cold and sheer fatigue. Once reaching the den, it probably cared not to venture forth until some of the crumbly deep snow had settled or melted, and it could travel about with more dignity befitting an impudent member of the red squirrel clan.

—December 16, 1982

Foxes Roam Bluffton Countryside

Foxes have holes, and the birds of the air have nests;
but the Son of man has nowhere to lay his head.
—Matthew 8:20

The gray fox pictured on the next page was well camouflaged against the mottled bark of the black walnut tree and the gray sky. It was acting rather coy as it nestled in the crotch of a tree near the Howard and Marcile Luginbuhl Habegger rural Bluffton home.

Another gray fox was hidden among the branches just above this one. When I climbed a step ladder to photograph the lower one, the other one seemed camera-shy, but it did not move much when I came within less than three feet of it. Below was a ditch full of snow and icy water. Perhaps it was loathe, as some cats I know, to get its feet wet, so it was reluctant to move.

The tree-climbing propensity of the gray fox is well known. No

Gray fox in black walnut tree

doubt these two sought the tree for their daily repose, for the next morning they had gone–probably to a drier spot where passerbys such as the Habeggers, Hiltys, and Henrys would not eye them.

•

Last December a pair of foxes were hanging around *Der Hof* on the Bluffton College Farm where Harvey and Alison Deckert Hiebert, and their daughter Jennifer, saw them. Perhaps an old woodchuck burrow was their haven in or close to the old orchard. They like to curl up in hollow trees but will not refuse the ready-made dens of badgers and groundhogs, or some holes in rocky ledges.

The gray fox, a lighter weight animal than it appears to be, weighs an average of nine and one-half pounds. Its diet is more variable than that of the red fox and includes insects, mice, rabbits, and an occasional bird, as well as wild fruits, acorns, and seeds.

We hoped the pair would stay around the old orchard where meadow mice should be plentiful, along with other staples of their diet. Perhaps they would sense they are on a wildlife preserve and have the friendly company of the Hieberts as their neighbors.

•

A red fox was staying recently in the vicinity of Fred and Annette Krehbiel Steiner's home near Bluffton. Probably its hide-away was nearby at the edge of a neighboring woods, for its range is said to be about a mile unless it is molested or harassed.

Although hunted vigorously in the area, a few of the dashing but shrewd red foxes manage to hold enough territory to survive and perpetuate their kind.

A helpful animal, the fox is a factor in keeping down the population of moles, deer mice, rabbits, and other animals. Without their help in controlling such animals, these prey could become serious pests to humans.

In spite of being persecuted by humans, the foxes will be with us to enliven the outdoor panorama if given half a chance to practice their winning ways as cunning hunters. Their faults are often imagined or grossly exaggerated, although in the eyes of their prey they are a menace whose presence is neither wanted nor appreciated.

•

Kit foxes are tiny editions of the fox family.

One Christmas Eve not many years ago, when I was visiting my brother Ralph in California, he and I were thrilled to see one of these tiny wise ones as we left Death Valley and were traveling toward Los Angeles on Highway 127.

The desert kit fox weighs about five pounds or less. It is equipped with long hairs on its feet that form "sand-sandals," enabling it to move swiftly and agilely over loose sand.

The kit fox's favorite bill-of-fare includes the kangaroo rat, which often cannot ambulate quickly enough to elude the little predator, if its haven is too far away in the brush.

It is a pity that these beautiful little foxes have been so mercilessly slaughtered. Their numbers now have decreased, to the detriment of the desert's beauty.

•

Was it a confrontation or just two different kinds of mammals getting acquainted? Or, perhaps, each was wondering just how an animal so different and more homely than itself could have come about and be allowed to exist.

Anyway, one night when Herman Hilty was driving on a country road by the home of Carl and Mildred Steiner Geiger in rural Bluffton, his car headlights shown upon a large raccoon and a red fox facing one another nose-to-nose. Being rudely interrupted by the vehicle, both turned tail–the masked one headed north and the sly one to the south. Whether or not the two renewed their rendezvous, we will never know. But for sure, Herman will not forget that instant—a scene that probably few mortals have been privileged to witness and enjoy.

–January 12, 1978

Beavers and Bugs by the Riverside

O Lord, how manifold are thy works!
In wisdom hast thou made them all;
the earth is full of thy creatures.
—Psalm 104:24

On a cold winter day I went for a walk along the North Canadian River near Spencer, Oklahoma, with my young friends James Mast and Michael Cothran. I was visiting James's parents, Moses and Sadie Swartzendruber Mast, and I was happy to have the two boys with me for my day's adventure.

We hadn't walked far when we encountered a number of trees that beavers had felled. Although they normally prefer poplars, these eager beavers appeared to take on any tree in the vicinity. In addition to the poplars, they had chiseled down ash-leafed maples (box elder), and even tried their logging skills on a tough black walnut tree having an 18-inch diameter. They didn't finish cutting this one—perhaps they gave up because of the tough fibers, or maybe they did not like the flavor of the bark. Anyway, they must have been satisfied with leaving their mark on this venerable old tree that had watched over the river for many years and probably had seen many generations of beavers come and go.

•

James and Michael seemed to find interesting nature material wherever they went.

When they stripped away an old piece of bark from a dead tree, they exposed some fascinating artwork of engraver beetles. The beetle trails led in every direction, marking intriguing designs in the wood. Some people have made a hobby of collecting these insect works of "art," even being able to identify the species of the insect artisan, much as a connoisseur of Goya's paintings is able to recognize the works of that master artist.

•

Inside a hollow log, the boys found evidence of garnering done by some small animal—perhaps a white-footed mouse or its close relative, the deer mouse. Tiny twigs had been gathered and the tender bark had been gnawed off the sticks, which left a green color on them as evidence of the original wrappings that had clothed the twigs.

The husks and shells of hickory and other nuts attested to the mice's patient labor spent gathering and shelling the nuts for winter use as well as for everyday needs. Inside the log, the animals were safe from the sharp eyes of hawks and owls constantly on the outlook for just such wild beasties. Dry leaves that could be shredded for soft bedding and nests for the young were also found in the fallen log.

A small spider, rudely disturbed by our actions, crawled from its silken cocoon. We left the cover intact so that the spider could later snuggle back into its cozy sleeping bag.

•

Under a rotten piece of wood partly frozen fast to the frosty ground, we found a mass of sow bugs, or "rolypolys" as Mike called them. Here in what would appear to us to be a very poor winter haven, the marble-shaped sow bugs must be able to survive winter's onslaughts.

Come warm weather, the tiny armadillo-like creatures will unroll their many pairs of legs and seek organic material among the moist layer of leaves where they will live out their days. We seldom see them unless they invade our gardens where they apparently feed on some of the vegetables we do not exactly care to share with them. But, even without our consent, they somehow manage to take their meager share, much to our dismay and futile efforts to evict them.

•

Draper Lake was the next stop. The boys were very familiar with the area where they were soon picking up "rock roses" along the red-sandstone beach.

Blackjack oak shared the uplands with patches of prairie, while blue jays, Carolina chickadees, titmice, cardinals, and slate-colored juncos found the area to their liking.

James and Mike gathered material for dry arrangements. They eagerly garnered colorful bluestem grass and twigs bearing the red berries of wahoo and buckbrush along with dry stalks and blossoms of pussytoes, goldenrod, and other inhabitants of the prairie patches.

When at home in Spencer, James skillfully arranged his materials in several vases–a fitting end to our day's adventure along the North Canadian River and Draper Lake.

–January 25, 1979

Opossum, snarling in the wind

The Quarry Has a Life of Its Own

Have you visited the treasuries of the snow...?
—Job 38:22a (Living Bible)

Although winter in Ohio can make us fuss and fume, our protests do no good. Even though this opossum may appear to be grinning from ear to ear, be assured that it is in no frame of mind to take any guff from anyone thinking of teasing or molesting the little marsupial during another February snowstorm.

•

Suspended from a mulberry twig by a slender cable of tough, twisted thread, a blob of pale chestnut shimmered dimly in February's murky haze. The distended spindle, swathed in layers of dusky fiber, was complacently swayed by the gentle nudgings of an idle breeze. Pasted on the surface were small, dried leaves that helped to camouflage the cocoon sheltering the pupa that may emerge in the spring to help perpetuate the species. For now, however, we will just have to wait for warmer weather.

•

For sure, the track pattern in snow along the trail leading down to the quarry was one that no cottontail or squirrel had printed. The footprints were not distinct in the deep coverlet, but a series of squiggles indicated that a muskrat had crossed the trail and headed for the ice-covered quarry.

I can't remember sighting any muskrats in the area, but they are known to wander extensively when driven by hunger or over-crowding. In this case, the musk-rat must have dragged its rubbery tail through cold and snow in hopes of finding shelter–an abandoned den or other such refuge. There, its frost-bitten rudder could thaw out before the animal proceeded onward. I hope the unhappy wanderer eventually found a territory suitable to its own needs and tastes.

•

Near the duck-feeding station on the limestone slabs by the water, there were signs of another client scrounging around for a few grains of corn left by the mallards.

The prints of a solitary rac-coon were plainly stamped in a limited edition near the feeding station. The pattern of the rear feet is similar to that of a human baby's foot.

Raccoons, like opossums and coyotes, are opportunistic feeders.

Of course, they have their "dru-thers," but they take what is available, and they seem to have gotten by through countless generations.

•

Today the quarry was in a grumpy mood, unlike several mornings earlier this winter when it was singing in a delightful fashion. Back then, the ice music burst forth with crystalline tinklings, zinging lightly and directly across the ice.

This present program, how-ever, was a rather stoic affair: grumblings, groanings, rumblings –somewhat like the uncouth gurg-lings of a steel barrel as its con-tents struggle out of the bunghole as though in painful birth.

Slightly resonant yet frankly unmusical, these sounds repre-sented only one of the moods created by the quarry from week to week, as though it had taken on a life of its own.

•

Many programs are dictated by the state of the quarry: ice cover, pattern of water–from calm to ripplings, to sullen disquiet, furious ragings, and even violence stirred by unrelenting winds attacking the defenseless waters.

Varieties of waterfowl seek the quarry as a rest stop: ducks, wild geese, mergansers, grebes, gulls of sundry denominations, all bobbing and rocking on the giant water bed that swells, bursts, and dashes according to the whims and moods of breeze, of wind, and of rain.

At times, the long, smooth waders of the great blue heron slowly stir the waters where frogs and fish hope to elude the spearfisher.

A kingfisher, rattling like a ratchet, zigzags across and along the quarry. It appears unable to make up its mind on what course to pursue. When it dives, it momentarily pierces the tough skin of the waters with its sharp beak, spears a fish and hauls it protesting from the water, spattering drops on the surface like a sprinkler on the rampage.

Such goings-on contribute to the life of our quarry.

−February 24, 1994

Along Smith Creek in Missouri

Then God looked over all that he had made, and it was excellent in every way.
−Genesis 1:31 (Living Bible)

On a brisk but sunny winter day in rural Versailles, Missouri, I went for a leisurely walk along Smith Creek with Norman and Mary Driver Wenger. Carefully making our way over packed ice that had resulted from a previous sleet storm, we noticed tracks of various animals that must have been foraging in the milo field.

Before we reached the creek we saw a shrike perched on a black willow. It was probably scanning the area for any movement that might indicate a meadow mouse darting swiftly and quietly from its hideaway in the milo field.

Later we saw another shrike near the Bethel Mennonite Church. These butcher birds, as they are sometimes called, reminded me of a poem Orlie J. King of Topeka, Indiana, shared with me some years ago:

I like the shrike−beak for a guillotine;
He does his work so slick and so clean;
His common sense must be immense!

•

Norman knew the area well, for it was where he and his brothers had helped their father, Jesse, work on the farm. Now Norman's brother, Roy, operates the farm and their father helps him.

As we picked our way along the creek bank, Mary remarked that she smelled sycamore. Now, the knowledge that sycamore had a smell was new to me, but when Mary crushed some dry leaves, the crumpled mass emitted a peculiar musky incense. She said that the globular seed-heads also possess this particular odor, which she could detect from a distance.

After this demonstration I will be on the lookout for the fragrance of this tree with its brown-and-white mottled bark whenever I roam in the woods or along streams where the sycamore prefers to grow.

Sycamore along Smith Creek, Versailles, Missouri

•

From among the dried plants lining the edge of the field, Mary gathered some specimens for her hobby of creating dried-plant designs. The silvery bracts of asters caught her attention, for she uses them along with goldenrod, ironweed bracts, butterprint (cottonweed, to Norman and Mary), and even a few rough seed heads of the cocklebur.

So, while listening to the sharp chirps of several cardinals and the shrill protestations of blue jays, we kept watching for plants suitable for creating intriguing and beautiful designs from material looked upon as useless by those unacquainted

with this type of art which Mary does so well.

•

Several marsh hawks were coursing back and forth over the fields and meadow. Like the shrike, the marsh hawks are alert to any sign of a mouse that may have strayed a bit too far from its burrow or hut.

Under some osage orange trees we came upon several interesting designs where squirrels had gnawed the upper half of some fruit that was frozen in the ice. We saw no squirrels, but undoubtedly some were nearby, sunning themselves on branches exposed to the warmth of a bright sun.

Seeing some buckbrush or coralberry plants with their clusters of red berries reminded me of those we enjoyed as children when we lived along Gypsum Creek in Saline County, Kansas. Opossums feed on the berries during the winter season when there are few insects or other summer food to be found.

•

Late in the evening I revisited the area. A male downy woodpecker drew my attention as he chipped away on a dead elm branch.

Many white-crowned sparrows flew into the shrubbery from the corner of a field where they were probably feasting on weed seed and milo grain.

Two shrikes continued their watchful vigil even as the last sunbeam faded when the sun slowly slipped below the horizon.

The shadows melted away and twilight began its brief reign. Finally, the muffled hoot of a barred owl sounded from somewhere in the southwest—ending an enjoyable day for me along Smith Creek on the Wenger farm in central Missouri.

—January 11, 1979

Storm Alert: Birds Flock to Feeders

Praise the Lord from the earth,
...fire and hail, snow and ice, gales of wind that obey his voice....
—Psalm 148:7-8 (Revised English Bible)

Premature darkness crept slowly over the landscape as snow clouds moved ominously across the sky. Small bits of shattered snowflakes were soon swirling over the ground. Small drifts of snow appeared–their forms continually changing–some disappearing as they merged with others. Soon no bare spots remained on lawns and streets.

As though responding to a storm alert, various species of birds appeared at the feeders. From an apple tree near the patio, a lone mourning dove cautiously surveyed the area before descending to a supply of grain below. Three others joined the first dove. Then, as though startled by real or imagined danger, they fled on whining wings back to the apple tree. There they waited amid the pelting snow. Soon, however, they flew back to the grain, feeding greedily on the emergency rations.

•

At another feeding station in Bluffton, stocked by Nelson and

Margaret Hahn Steiner, an exciting happening resulted from the snowstorm. A flock of 30 elegant grosbeaks descended on the Steiner avian smorgasbord. Soon showers of sunflower hulls were flying from the birds' powerful snipping machines, while the tender kernels were methodically conveyed down the hatches of the hungry birds.

The Steiners were also favored by the presence of a small flock of pine siskins. Moreover, a friendly company of goldfinches in their subdued finery added extra excitement to the outdoor panorama.

•

A day or so later, Harvey and Alison Deckert Hiebert saw a half-dozen bobwhite quail. The birds were busily harvesting seed from grass that protruded from the snow at the Bluffton College Farm where Peter and Elizabeth Burkholder Thut and their family lived over a century ago.

A family of pheasants, consisting of six females and two gaily-dressed males, crossed the Hiebert yard and disappeared into the old orchard. Their feed must have been hard to come by, as snow covered much of their usual food supply.

A flock of about 55 Canada geese was using the ice-covered pond as their nighttime resting place until just after the storm. Last seen on December 6, they

may have made their way southward where the living would be a bit easier.

•

A sassy mob of blue jays was obviously interested and rather displeased with something in the large tree just outside Elmer and Florence Krites Nusbaum's house near Bluffton. Florence guessed that perhaps the screech owl that had occupied a hollow in the tree for several years was back. Sure enough, a few days later, at dusk, she saw the little tuft-eared owl peeking from the hole.

The jays had reason to pester the owl, for bluejays are sometimes included in the little owl's diet, although mice are a more common item on its shopping list. The Nusbaum bird feeding station is just below the owl's comfy cavern. Therefore the over-inquisitive or foolish bird that goes beyond the limits of common sense may wind up as food for the owl, a bird that thoroughly disdains the bill of fare offered at the feeding stations. The owl, however, would not refuse to dine on a customer if given a chance.

•

A slate-colored junco demonstrated its skill at finding food when snow covers much of its natural sources. It stood on a snowdrift and carefully picked at seeds from the heads of a brown-eyed Susan, as the blustery wind caused the plant to trace designs in the snow.

Then, as a song sparrow sang as though its calendar was confused, the junco flew to a prairie sunflower and coaxed kernels from the small disks of seeds swaying in the frigid wind. Later the junco perched on the stem of a pigweed and pecked at the plume filled with black seeds.

So, although the gardener's failure to practice "clean farming" might have earned him a poor rating by members of the green thumb fraternity, such birds as the junco would probably rate him otherwise. Anyway, these unpulled plants served the junco well, while the gardener was rewarded by the presence of the industrious little finch.

—December 22, 1977

Part II

Spring

Pussy willow bouquets

Pussy Willow Debut Is Not Far Off

*He dawns on them like the morning light,
like the sun shining forth upon a cloudless morning,
like the rain that makes grass to sprout from the earth.*
—II Samuel 23:4

Soon, here in Ohio, the smooth, shiny buds of the pussy willow, *Salix discolor,* will respond to the February sunshine and slight mellowing of the winter weather. Then the soft, silky puffs or catkins will be glowing even a month before spring arrives. Honeybees will flock around the golden bouquets and stuff crumbs of pollen into the tiny bags provided as handy baskets on their hind legs.

Pussy willow switches strung with silvery catkins are popular at this time of the year when the air is frigid and the ground snow-covered. Many people fill containers with the cut canes and display them where their beauty can be seen, for hope is kindled as the arrival of spring seems just around the corner.

By January 28, several of the pussy willow trees in our yard were already showing flecks of cotton, so it shouldn't be long before the pussy willow debut will take place here in northwestern Ohio.

•

Willow buds are choice food for a number of our wildlife species.

Here in Ohio, buds and tender twig tips are sought after by gray and red foxes; we have both species in the Bluffton-Pandora area. Tender canes with their buds are relished by moose, elk, deer, rabbits, beaver, wood rats, meadow mice, and other wildlife.

On the tundra above Rocky Mountain Mennonite Camp near Divide, Colorado, white-tailed ptarmigans, sheltering themselves from strong, icy winds during winter, seek out and dine on the nutritious buds of the dwarfed willows found in the snowdrifts in which the hardy birds protect themselves. Some of the willows on the tundra only reach a height of six inches or less, with the bulk of the plant anchored underground.

•

The flexible switches of certain willows were once commonly used in making baskets.

More than 100 species are native to North America, and more than 300 species are distributed over the world, mostly in the northern parts, making important contributions to wildlife and aiding in prevention of soil erosion along the streams and waterways of the world.

—February 11, 1988

Spring Awakens in Northwestern Ohio

For the winter is past, the rain is over and gone.
The flowers are springing up and the time of the singing of birds has come.
Yes, spring is here.
　　　　　　　　　　　—Song of Solomon 2:11-12 (Living Bible)

While touring the Bluffton College Nature Preserve on a cold, wet day in March, my guest Sharon Snyder and I saw the tracks of a pheasant in the snow. We followed the footprints that led in a straight line toward the entrance of the South Woods. We turned left into the moist gloom of the woods and slowly tramped the crisp trail paved with wood chips. Even the winter birds kept their conversations to a minimum, with hardly a spirited peep from the ever-present downy woodpecker. An occasional tapping of the little carpenter was heard, but no utterances whatsoever.

As we walked along the east fork of the trail, I thought I caught the faint sound of a bubbling stream. Surely, I thought, there is no stream here, so I must be letting my imagination run wild and free. So, I summarily dismissed the matter.

While we were returning along the west fork, I was almost sure again that I heard the babble of a stream. Then, Sharon exclaimed, "Where is that sound of water coming from?" When we moved a bit on the trail, sure enough, we heard a gurgling at the edge. Then it became clear that our weight on the ice, covering puddles of water under the wood chips, forced the water to gush out with a gurgle. So the case of the mysterious babbling brook was solved, and the soundness of my hearing was vindicated.

—April 8, 1993

•

With the first day of spring having arrived, we find our weather in a state of hesitant transition.

During visits to the homes of Ted and Gayle Gerber Koontz in Everett, Massachusetts, and Gordon and Dorothy Krehbiel Kaufman in Lexington, I noted how this process unfolded as I marvelled at the abundant for-sythia in the early spring. The brightness of the yellow-gold flowers of hedges and large clumps was a delight to the eyes. Somehow, in spite of, or perhaps because of, the harsh winter, they seemed anxious to put on a more impressive performance than usual. Sunny days and cool nights probably influenced them to appear in their best attire during their lengthened show season which was still too brief for those of us who enjoy and appreciate the golden bells of early spring.

James Fenimore Cooper, writing in his book, *The Pioneers*, back in 1823, described this fluctuation in Central New York in this manner:

"As the spring gradually approached, the immense piles of snow, by alternate thaws and frosts, and repeated storms, had obtained a firmness which threatened a tiresome durability, began to yield to the influence of milder breezes and a warmer sun. The gates of heaven at times seemed to open, and a bland air diffused itself over the earth, when animate and inanimate nature would awaken, and for a few hours, the gaiety of spring shone in every eye, and smiled on every field."

And indeed it is often so out here in Northwestern Ohio.

—June 29, 1978

Grief and Reassurance Before the Dawn

Weeping may tarry for the night, but joy comes with the morning.
—Psalm 30:5

Blessed are the peacemakers, for they shall be called children of God.
—Matthew 5:9

At 4:30 that March morning, there were no signs of dawning as a surly, 25-degree wind bluffed its way through the treetops along the dyke of the National Quarry. A somber day was likely.

I had just negotiated a bend when out of thick darkness emerged the resonant murmur of a gang of mallard drakes, probably secluded near the quarry's west bank.

Strangely, the hen ducks, who usually greet me with loud quacking, were not to be heard. Perhaps they were unaware of my presence—or possibly, in subdued asperate tones and with heads nodding, they commented quietly to one another on my appearance at such an inconvenient and foreboding hour.

Moments earlier, the intimate chatter of the males seemed to come from over the bank in Riley Creek. Perhaps it appeared so due to some disorientation on my part as I walked cautiously, rather disquieted, along the indistinct winding trail. It was now only a dappled blur between the darker tree presence—sensed perhaps as much as seen.

A different revelation came from a series of slender, whistled notes of short duration. No doubt, a gathering of ducks of a different tongue and persuasion was bunched among them.

Through a band of light shining across the quarry from the east, indistinct forms bobbed amid the lively dancing of the twinkling wavelets. Each indistinct phantom quickly melted away, paddling into the darker portion of black water to the south.

•

Troubled thoughts had kept me awake that early morning. I agonized over what the media hailed as "victory" and "peace" following the human slaughter in the Persian Gulf. Mourning for the victims of that carnage led me to my personal grief over the loss of our son, Larry, and three of our friends in a plane crash near Ottawa, Ohio, in early October.

Those four men were victims of an accident, not as a result of an intentional operation. Had they lost their lives in the prosecution of a war planned and executed by others, and without their consent, I'm sure that anger would have been added to my grief.

But then, what about the thousands of children, women, men, whose lives have been snuffed out, their homes destroyed, their way of life disrupted, their fields, gardens, and pleasant plantings made a ruin? Are these not also my other children, my grandchildren, my kinfolk with lives and souls just as precious though thousands of miles from my blood-relatives here?

I was angry, grief-stricken, feeling powerless, gripped by the terrible sin of war: the cruelty, the planned killing and maiming, the desolation of homes of fellow human beings having the same dreams as those of my family and friends, the pitiless exaltation of the "victors" and their boasting.

•

Along the darkened trail that morning, I remembered the words of Jesus: "You have heard that it was said, 'You shall love your neighbor and hate you enemy.' But I say to you, love your enemies."

Returning along the dyke, a sudden scrambling noise...a bit startling as some animal scurried for even darker cover down the bank of the Riley. No over-eager redbird had yet broken into the early morning hour with its energetic, "What cheer! What cheer"...What cheer?

But the Lord's words were there, "Blessed are the peacemakers, for they shall be called the children of God!" Reassuring. Helpful. Encouraging, too, his confident, "Blessed are those who mourn, for they shall be comforted."

Grateful am I for the church—for a fellowship of the merciful who grieve with us and for us, praying, sacrificing, loving—a peacemaking community of caring people all over God's world. Amen!

—*March 21, 1991*

•

October 18, 1990—MWR Editor's note: *Roy Henry's son Larry, 37, died October 7 in a plane crash. The Review staff extend our sympathies and prayers to the Henry family in this time of loss.*

American elm near Mulberry Grove, Illinois

Elm Buds Good For Squirrels or People

Praise the Lord from the earth....
Mountains and all hills, fruit trees and all cedars!
                              —Psalm 148:7,9

The elegance of its design makes our American elm, *ulmus americanas*, a favorite of many people. This lovely elm had plenty of elbow room in which to develop its naturally graceful, feather-duster form.

Unfortunately, most of our larger, older American elms have been killed off by the Dutch elm disease, which is carried by a bark beetle, and a spreading elm like this one is becoming a rare sight in many places.

Along a country road past my boyhood home north of Gypsum, along Gypsum Creek in Kansas, there was a beautiful American elm. My father, Edward, mentioned that if the tree could be transplanted to a house yard it would be worth hundreds of dollars. That was way back in the 1920s when the dollar was worth many times more than it is today; I am pleased to remember that Dad saw the aesthetic value of this tree which too often goes unnoticed by the passerby and is thought of as "only a tree."

•

Elm seeds and swollen buds in the spring are food for gray and fox squirrels as well as opossums. Bobwhite, grouse, and other birds feed on them also. I first sampled the swollen buds some years ago and was surprised at the flavor, which reminded me of black walnut meats. That stage passes rapidly, and the tender twigs are eagerly browsed by deer and rabbits.

Early settlers stripped the bark, soaked it, then used the fiber for chair bottoms. Native Americans used the bark of the elm tree to make fiber for rope.

Elm wood is hard to split; it is hard and tough, and was used for products that demanded these qualities. Hubs of wheels, saddle trees, barrel hoops, and veneer for baskets and crates were made from the elm. However, the most valuable quality of the American elm, was its grace and form, grown in open spaces where its natural design could develop.

–March 27, 1986

Wildlife at the Cullar Farm in Ohio

He placed springs in the valleys,
and streams that gush from the mountains.
They give water for all the animals to drink.
...and the birds nest beside the streams
and sing among the branches of the trees.
   —Psalm 104:10-12 (Living Bible)

This fledgling bronzed grackle seems to be unsure of the fellow with the black box.

In a hedge of honeysuckle and conifers at the John and Lillie Goering Cullar home in North Lima, Ohio, the parents of a clutch of youngsters were noisily protesting my presence near their nesting tree. To accommodate them, I soon left the immediate area.

Out in a nearby plot, an adult song sparrow flew from one dried

Bronzed grackle fledgling

stalk to another, not caring, it seemed, to reveal its nesting site somewhere in the vicinity. A beakload of what appeared to be grayish "worms," (perhaps cutworms or armyworms) was all ready to be served to the nestling as soon as the intruder left the area. Shortly, I retreated in order to permit the little finch to perform her domestic duties without interference.

•

Toward evening when John and I were walking along a road bordering the Cullar farm, John sighted three deer in a nearby marshy area.

The two smaller deer seemed especially inquisitive. They watched us a few moments–their ears like miniature radar receivers. Suddenly their curiosity evidently overcame their caution and they moved quickly toward us. Soon they were at the roadside, only about 150 feet from where John and I were standing.

The doe hesitated briefly, then ran quickly and deliberately toward us, stomped the hard road a resounding thump, and leaped across the ditch into the field beyond. Apparently she had taken enough foolhardly behavior from the two youngsters and decided it was high time to get the curious duo out of possible danger.

Evidently the two young deer must have known she meant business; they instantly followed her into the field and disappeared.

•

Judging by the number of tracks in the area, it must be good country for white-tailed deer, the most abundant deer species found in the U.S.

One Sunday morning, John and Lillie were treated to an especially interesting sight. Out in a nearby field, eight deer were feeding in plain view. It isn't often that people get the privilege of seeing such a large family of deer practically in their own front yard.

–June 28, 1980

Birds in the Neighborhood

There shall the owl nest and lay and hatch and gather her young in her shadow....
      —Isaiah 34:15

For a number of weeks, a rare visitor from the tundra has been spending its time here in the Bluffton community. I first saw the huge white snowy owl in a plowed field just east of town.

Sitting there on some large clods, the snowy owl seemed at ease as it must appear on hummocks in the Artic tundra of Alaska or Greenland. As it flew to several other positions, it did so without any signs of injury.

Why it would choose to remain here so far from its homeland for such a long period into late spring is a mystery. The usual reason for their migration southwards during certain winters is that a sharp decline in the number of food sources such as arctic hares, lemmings, and other rodents in their homelands sends them seeking food elsewhere.

•

Here in Ohio the first record of an invasion of snowies was in the winter of 1858-59. This flight occurred at Cleveland, according to Peterjohn in his *Birds of Ohio*.

Snowy owl: visitor from the far north

During this century, large flights of snowies have been recorded, with a remarkable number tallied for the winter of 1941-42. From the Cleveland area, 100 to 150 were reported; lower counts were made from other parts of the state. If this owl remains here into June, that may set a record for confirmed late sightings in Ohio.

For most people in our community who saw this snowy owl, it was their first sighting of the species. Its presence among us has caused much delight and ex- citement. It is indeed quite an experience to watch the great white predator as it surveys the area from high above ground at the top of the Arby's sign along Highway 103 just east of Bluffton.

•

A downy woodpecker must regard the booster box on a TV aerial as an ideal sounding board for signals notifying its neighbors that it has a claim to that area.

At the home of Darwin and Evelyn Johnson Lugibuhl south of Bluffton, the little carpenter has refused to be dissuaded from using the small metal box to signal its sole rights to the area.

Darwin decided to encourage the little fellow to lay off its early-morning tattoo sessions. He first tried putting a stick at the spot, hoping the downy would make the switch to the wooden pole. "No way!" responded the woodpecker, as it continued to tap away on the little steel canister.

Then Darwin reported another stratagem to convince Tommy Woodpecker to do his signalling from some other spot. He attached a cloth close to the box, thinking the fluttering flag might distract and perhaps disturb the hard-headed bird to the point where it would desert that signal station. Again, the little black and white tapper, with a solemn tip of the head, responded with, "No, thank you!" and continued beating away at the metal box.

At that point, Darwin decided, "If you can't whip 'em, join 'em!" So he removed the pole and banner. He now hopes he will learn to appreciate the percussion performances as the tiny woodpecker continues to drum away in apparent assurance that his system is working and his territory secure.

Meanwhile Darwin and Evelyn are trying to be cool, real cool, as Tommy Woodpecker bangs away in the most resolute fashion. And he does have rythm, a rather smooth beat that the Lugibuhls just might learn to appreciate in due time...after so many years.

•

At Walden Hilty's home in rural Pandora, a pair of house finches apparently decided to build their nest where the living would be easy as well as secure.

Waldon had recently hung a fine new feeder close to the house. It has a bowl-like receptacle for the seeds and an inverted bowl as a cover to protect the feed from rain. The provident finches constructed their nest smack dab in the middle of the receptacle containing the sunflower seeds.

A cowbird also found the location favorable and laid its egg there among the four finch eggs. We removed the cowbird's unsolicited contribution and hoped that the legitimate eggs would be incubated successfully. With the nest surrounded by sunflower seeds, the finch parents should have no trouble feeding their future fledglings.

—*June 11, 1992*

Frog Creatures Great and Small

Let the field be joyful, and all that is in it.
—Psalm 96:12a (New King James)

In Bryant's, "To a Waterfowl," the following lines could apply to cricket frogs as well as to waterfowl: "Seek'st thou the plashy brink. Of weedy lake, or marge of river wide...?"

Our tiny one-inch froggies prefer plant-fringed farm ponds, lazy, green-bordered pasture streams, and other watery places edged by sleek water plantain, reeds, rushes, and other greenery. There they can quickly leap for cover whenever raccoons, snakes, and herons come seeking a quickie lunch in the quiet of the lovely countryside.

The voice of the cricket frog is similar to the clack of two pebbles being struck together. A chorus of the lively wee ones is quite a performance; the stutterings can be heard over quite a distance–rather pleasant music to my noncritical ears.

As children, whenever we walked along a meandering pasture stream, the clacking of cricket frogs reminded us of the tapping of tiny hammers in the hands of elves and goblins. At that time, we did not associate the sound with the little frogs that quickly hopped for cover as

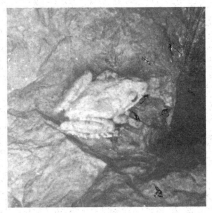

Cricket frog

we moved slowly along the pasture brook. We were fascinated with the exciting prospect of coming upon an elf mending shoes in a tiny workshop among the rushes. We preferred to think that the clicks heard in the vegetation were the tapping of fairy creatures, rather than to know the real source of the mysterious, enchanting crepitations.

•

At our country grade school near Gypsum, Kansas, we learned to sing a delightful song about twenty froggies:

Twenty froggies went to school,
Down beside a rushy pool.
Twenty little coats of green,
Twenty vests so white and clean.
"We must be on time," said they;

"First we study, then we play.
That is how we keep the rule,
When we froggies go to school!"
And, no doubt, that's exactly what they did. Bless 'em!

—April 8, 1993

•

In the marshy areas around the Cullar farm at North Lima, evening brought out several choruses who were members of the Amphibian A Cappella Choirs.

Singing a cappella in what appeared to be a very accomplished manner were choruses of spring peepers. The tinkling notes, very delightfully rendered, became a crescendo as shadows lengthened over their several staging areas. During infrequent intervals of silence, a lone peeper would sound forth as though he had missed a cue, or else was showing off what he might have considered a superior tenor solovoice. Perhaps he was right, for who was I to judge the vocal merits of a member of the frog fraternity!

•

Tiny chorus frogs, not to be outdone by their piping neighbors, sounded forth with their more intricate vocal score. With apparent gusto and frogonian finesse, they perform their thumb-rubbed-over-a-comb-rendition of what must be a primitive expression of "ye olde days beyond batrachian recall."

Anyway, amid the blossoming spring cress and the rounded puffball seed heads of medicinal coltsfoot, their concerts went on. The nocturnal performances were doubtlessly enjoyed by the tribes involved, as well as by those of us who appreciate their fascinating vocal endeavors.

—June 28, 1980

•

By April, the song and clamor of frogs is in full swing over much of our land. But here in northwest Ohio I have heard the chorus frogs in concert as early as March 24. On January 15, 1978, Edward and Katherine Weins Dettweiler heard a toad calling—for whatever reason—at their home in Reedley, California. Evidently the calendar meant little to the toad, who had probably been soaked the night before by a heavy rain that had continued much of the night.

But it was a bit late for Woody the wood frog to be in song last August near Round Lake Outpost at Camp Friedenswald in Michigan. Although he was quiet, Woody was frognapped by Rodney Dyck, Bluffton, Ohio, and held for identification. I had first met up with a wood frog at what we called O.J. Yoder's woods near Topeka, Indiana, about 20 years ago. Woody was a beautiful frog with a bronzy skin color that sometimes turned to a burnished pinkish hue.

Woody the wood frog

Rana sylvatica ranges farther north than any other North American amphibian or reptile species. It has been found in Alaska and in shallow tundra pools of the Far North. Northern specimens assume more of the features of a toad, for they have heavier legs and an overall stouter form. However, our Woody was a sleek creature as the photo clearly shows.

•

Woodrow the wood frog was given a temporary home at our place in order for me to get some mug shots of the handsome amphibian. I had planned to release him when I attended a retreat at Camp Friedenswald, his home site, but the retreat was canceled. That left me with the unenviable responsibility of bedding and boarding the bronze beauty for an indefinite period.

Because Woodrow did not take too enthusiastically to a leash, I found myself assigned to do his hopping and hunting for him. That, my dear friends, was at times no little, or laughing, matter. A frogherd I was not cut out to be, but the task did get me outdoors, where I met all kinds of critters, such as robins, grackles, and starlings, seriously engaged in the art of hunting.

I encountered other interesting hunters and gatherers, including rove beetles, tiger beetles, wasps, and bees, as well as crab, wolf, and jumping spiders of sundry sorts. On a few occasions I came upon a skulking assassin bug or a praying mantid apparently waiting for their prey to come to them. But I had to get on with my hunting chores.

Eventually, through patience and stealth, I stalked and captured a number of small lawn crickets. Woody quickly dispatched one after another to a limit of four. But they did not necessarily disappear in a flash after his quick lunge and deft flick of the tongue. Sometimes the jumping-jack legs of the formerly light-hearted insects would protrude from the corners of the amphibian's ample mouth. Soon, however, the legs, too, would vanish, but the smile remained on the face of Woody the frog.

Woody also accepted wiggly earthworms as though accustomed to that bill-of-fare. In a fairly short time he was able to consume a few, spending more time working the larger ones down the hatch. If one lingered, he merely waited until batrachian digestion took care of the problem.

I wonder if Woody would have taken such a liking to the earthworms which Carl Lehman says are numerous during the rainy season in Botswana in Africa. They are black and very obvious in the area of Mahalapye after a hard rain, much like our common nightcrawlers.

In fact, I wonder what Woody would have done if he were tossed a large nightcrawler to chaw on. But we know that the giant earthworms found in the Andes of Colombia from 13,000 to 14,000 feet would hold no temptation for Woody or any of our frogs in search of a meal. For these three-to-five-feet long squirming mammoth creatures, sometimes over two inches in diameter would send Woody scurrying for little red wigglers, if he had a hankering for earthworms he could handle. One wouldn't fault him for that.

And Woody would be at the prey end of the predator-prey action if he met up with the giant frog of Rio Muni and Cameroon in West Africa. *Conraua goliath* is the largest of the over 600 species of true frogs in the world. It can weigh more than seven pounds, with a head and body length of about 12 inches. As food, Woodrow would appear a tiny tidbit or animated crumb to his colossal cousin from West Africa.

—April 22, 1982

"Toady Woodhouse" Welcome in Garden

O, Lord, what a variety you have made!
And in wisdom you have made them all!
—Psalm 104:24a (Living Bible)

This all-set-to-go garden toad doesn't look like he'll take any guff from anyone, not even from a dog that is green enough to think he can grab Toady and get away with it.

I remember way back when we lived on a farm in Saline County, Kansas, our dog tried to get a mouthful of a congenial toad. It didn't take long for the poison in the toad's chemically-treated coveralls to take effect on the foolhardy pooch. Frothing at the mouth, our hound dog, who didn't know the difference between a toad and a frog, kept shaking his head as if trying to rid himself of the empty noggin that had gotten him into trouble. He had quite a hard time trying to spew out of his mouth what must have been a very unpleasant dose of mongrel-mace.

One thing is for sure: old Teddy probably never touched another innocent toad again. He was no doubt content to just watch the portly insect eradicator go about as a peaceful member of the toad clan living along Gypsum Creek.

And by the way, Toady Woodhouse, *Bufo woodhousei*, is a true

Toady Woodhouse

Jayhawker. He was toad-napped for a mug shot from the Tilmar and Evelyn Schrock Kaufman farm near Moundridge, Kansas.

•

Did you know it rained toads? At least that is what we were told as kids living along Gypsum Creek.

And at times it did look a bit like the saying was true, at least for me, a skinny young lad of perhaps seven years. It took on a hint of fact when after a rain, we once saw our sandy loam yard and garden fairly pulsating with tiny toadlets.

I can well recall this happening after a summer rain. West of our house a number of these wee ones were taking mini-hops across the walk, just as though they were really fresh from heaven and rinsed by a sweet-smelling shower. Of course, insects hunted down by the cute little toadfrogs would have another name for the origin of their plump pursuers, for Toady's tribe stands second to none as insect eradicators. Cheers for Toady Woodhouse and his kin —may their tribe increase!

•

And what about toads causing warts?

I knew of no boys who were afraid to pick up a toad and handle it. Even though we were told that the toad's wetting solution would cause warts to grow on our hands, we weren't very cautious when washing up after touching the amiable amphibians.

Whenever we acquired warts, I suppose the thought passed our minds, but such thoughts never stopped us from catching the likable fellows.

•

Even William Shakespeare passed along a thought about toads that his actors could proclaim. He records that a toad carries a jewel in its head—what a nice thought. And farmers and gardeners would agree that the toad is indeed a jewel when it comes to destroying insects around the place.

One autumn day we were favored by a toad who was apparently looking over our property here in Bluffton. I hurried to find a fine, soft, dug-up spot in our flower garden. I hoped that the toad would bury itself there for the winter and emerge in the spring to go about its job of ridding our garden of insect enemies. Of course, we preferred that the chap be a discerning fellow who would refrain from munching on our friends, the ladybird beetles, who keep busy gobbling up the green aphids that can be real pests in the garden.

To date, I have not seen our friend, but one thing is clear: if it is in our garden, it will be doing us a great favor at no charge whatever. Yes, indeedy, Toady Woodhouse and his friends will be plenty welcome here.

—*May 22, 1986*

Pasture and Smith River at Milverton, Ontario

A Stroll on an Ontario Farm

He...makes grass grow upon the hills.
He gives to the beasts their food, and to the young ravens which cry.
—Psalm 147:8-9

It was already early evening when I left the home of David and Levina Kuepfer Jantzi for a stroll on the John Oesche farm at Milverton, Ontario.

A startled cottontail sped northward past the old C&R railroad station, while a scattering of white-crowned sparrows calmly held their positions along a fence-row and continued to whistle their pleasant notes for whatever reasons they do so.

My destination was a pasture where a delightful little stream, Smith River, wound its way in a rather carefree fashion, uninhibited by steep banks and timber.

•

On a smooth boulder at the water's edge, a song sparrow with fancy dark breast-pin hopped about, as the stream leisurely sidled past on its way southward.

Shells of freshwater clams, perhaps picked clean by raccoons near the northern limit of their range, lay in the shallow water. Tiny minnows flashed in the riffles, some leaping out as though evading larger members of their clan who had no respect for smaller relatives during the dinner hour. Others had probably been plucked from their midst by a kingfisher that flew from the site in an erratic course upstream, chortling as it went.

A water strider shuffled onto the polished top of a water lily and clumsily hobbled off again, leaving a small puddle of water on the lily's table-top surface. Dark dimples appeared where the strider's skis touched the smooth waterskin arena. There the water strider displayed its skill, chasing its prey and performing thrilling ski routines while staying alert to dangers from below.

•

East of the river, a large sugar maple and a scaly-barked elm dominated the scene. At the foot of the elm lay a large stone curiously carved by water. Nearby, a clump of scrawny wild black cherry saplings had been stripped bare by an encampment of tent caterpillars whose mother had chosen their campsite well.

Protected by clumps of thorny haws and boulders, a few large-flowered trilliums and fawn lilies had managed to survive and grace the pasture by their presence.

Small blocks of pussytoes were at home on the higher ground where the woodchuck had its den

among the boulders. Here, too, meadowlarks whistled and goldfinches flashed their golden finery in innocent and uninhibited display as they dipped and chirped in the sunshine.

•

Back again at the stream, I examined a cluster of speedwells growing out of the packed soil near a trail. Only by close scrutiny could an observer appreciate the delicate china-like blossoms with thin, blue stripes exquisitely etched on the light-blue background of the fragile petals.

As the sun was setting, a killdeer gave a sudden, startling cry as though its nest was being approached too closely for it to remain calm any longer.

A series of huge waves wrinkled the surface of Smith River as a large fish—perhaps a carp—madly zig-zagged downstream toward the bridge. A starling, resembling a sailing triangle, headed northwest as though on serious business, while a lone pigeon flew directly toward town. A dog barked in the distance as the chill of approaching night slowly settled down like some giant electric blanket with controls in reverse.

•

From the bridge on Mill Street, I spied a calico cat which had a white stripe that began on its forehead and fanned out into a white facial napkin. At first the feline sat motionless in the meadow to the south. Then it moved down to the base of a huge willow where it watched the observer, its white front paws contrasting with the dark, damp soil on which it sat.

A shore bird, now invisible in the shadow of the shoreline, emitted a slightly musical "peet peet peet!" To me, the bird sounded as though it was in mild agony, although it probably felt that its solo was a superb performance –and perhaps it was.

By this time I had come full circle and approached the Jantzi residence just as Levina left the garden with a supply of fresh rhubarb. In a short time I had witnessed many wayside goings-on along Smith River at Milverton which, by now, was much more to me than just another town in southern Ontario.

–June 9, 1977

Squirrels From East to West

These all look to thee, to give them their food in due season.
When thou givest to them, they gather it up;
when thou openest thy hand, they are filled with good things.
—Psalm 104:27-28

By its plump figure one could conclude that this portly fox squirrel has had a good season of handouts.

It and others were common in one of the city parks in Fresno, California, several years ago when my brother Ray introduced me to that park with its friendly squirrels and street-wise pigeons.

Although *Sciurus niger*, the eastern fox squirrel, is not a native west of the Rocky Mountains, it has been introduced into a number of cities including Fres-

Fox Squirrel at Fresno, California

no, Sacramento, San Francisco, and Seattle. If the squirrels are as contented as this one appears to be, we might conclude they are doing well in the areas where they have been settled.

•

Walking a utility tight-rope with no safety net beneath can be dangerous even for the nimble fox squirrel.

When we lived on North Main Street, in Newton, Kansas, I witnessed a tight-rope happening that could have resulted in a fatality for a nervy fox squirrel who must have chosen to live dangerously.

The confident squirrel was loping along the cable looking neither to the right nor the left, apparently going about its squirrel business like a good citizen. Suddenly a pair of crows appeared on the scene and immediately proceeded to apply the old dive-bomb treatment, a favorite diversion for members of the crow family. They almost upset the frightened squirrel who was desperately trying to reach the utility pole.

When the squirrel finally reached the pole it sat there a few minutes as though contemplating its close brush with a fatal accident.

•

A gray squirrel was taking his own sweet time crossing Cherry Street, here in Bluffton. His nonchalance quickly turned to panic when without warning a blackbird swooped from out of nowhere and attacked him from the rear. Not a trace of dignity or grace was exhibited by the terror-stricken *Sciurus carolinensis* as it scrambled in desperate disarray up the nearest tree. Too befuddled to chatter a nasty retort, the panting squirrel just sat and stared with bulging eyes. As for the grackle, one could imagine this reaction, "Now this just about makes my day!"

•

My brother Ralph and I were hiking up a slope of San Jacinto Peak in California when we stopped at about a 7,300-ft. elevation. We were attracted to a squirrel perched on a pine branch. It was a messy-looking western gray squirrel contentedly munching on a pine seed from a goopy cone held in its gummy paws. *Sciurus griseus* was working at reaching the seeds inside the green, sticky cone.

And was it a sorrowful sight! It looked like a mink stole that had been run through a washing machine and thrown across a fence to dry! However, the seeds must have been quite tasty to entice the squirrel to get its fur stuck together with the glue-like resin of the cone.

Anyway, who are we to fault the squirrels even though they may have to work hours in order to clean their coats of the sticky resin.

•

Once when we went on vacation, we left a salt bag filled with a goodly number of black walnuts on our patio. Upon returning we were surprised to find the bag open and dozens of walnut shells scattered around the patio.

Later when I cracked some of the abandoned walnuts I found they were all empty. Not a single walnut left by the squirrels was filled with nutmeats. Like the experts at fairs and carnivals who are often successful at guessing the weight of passersby, the bushytails can evidently lift a walnut and tell by its weight if it is worth opening or storing for the winter.

–May 14, 1981

Killdeer Protects Eggs with Trickery

If you chance to come upon a bird's nest, in any tree or on the ground, with young ones or eggs and the mother sitting upon the young or upon the eggs, you shall not take the mother with the young....

–Deuteronomy 22:6

I was eager to follow up on a telephone call that Ruth Sommers Augsburger had made in my absence from home. Checking with her soon after my return, I hurried to the Augsburger farm a few miles from Bluffton.

Ruth told me that a pair of killdeer plovers recently had been engaged in some peculiar goings-on at the site of a burned building. By their injury-feigning performances, we suspected a nest was nearby.

Long ago on a farm in Kansas, I had found a killdeer nest and later, in the same field,

Killdeer Plover with nest

saw a downy young bird running among the furrows and ridges of our sorghum field. Ever since then I had wanted the opportunity to photograph a killdeer with its nest, eggs, and young fledglings. So this appeared to be a

Eggs of killdeer plover, Augsburger Farm, Bluffton, Ohio

possible golden opportunity to realize my objective, and I was excited at the prospect.

•

Ruth, an accomplished imitator of birds songs, has given many programs based on this rare talent. I had heard her perform several times and had always admired and appreciated her skill as she went through her routine, imitating the calls and songs of familiar birds: robins, cardinals, chickadees, bobwhite quail, red-tailed hawk, and many more.

By whistling imitations of the sharp calls of "Killdee! Killdee!" Ruth had been communicating with the pair, so they were already somewhat conditioned to her presence. We would just have to see how they would respond with a stranger in their area. I hoped for the best.

•

With camera in hand, I approached the killdeer slowly and cautiously so as not to unduly disturb the bird, hoping to get some fairly close-up photos. Then, too, I was intently examining the ground before inching my way along, for it is easy to overlook the well-camouflaged nest and eggs of this clever plover.

To my surprise and delight, the "chattering plover," as it is sometimes called, permitted me to approach within four or five feet from where she stood, feigning injury by tilting her wing to the ground, calling, but not moving an inch from her position among the cinders.

Suddenly Ruth called out, "It's right there. She's standing by the nest!"

Sure enough, having been concentrating on the bird and looking closely at the ground immediately ahead before moving forward, we had overlooked the obvious. For the nest was a mere scrape in the soil and was un-lined except for a few larger cinders–certainly not the nice soft pad one might expect to cushion the four large, handsomely spotted eggs cleverly blending in with the ash and cinder sur-roundings.

Apparently Ruth's previous contacts with the pair caused this adult to refuse to continue the injury-feigning routine at the nest, although a few minutes later, away from the eggs, the poor bird was dragging itself along as though its wing was broken. But we quickly left the site and wondered where the other bird was, for it did not ap-pear during the few minutes we were there.

I knew that the parents took turns incubating the eggs, so I thought that perhaps the spouse was away, hunting food while its mate guarded the nest. At any rate, we hope both adult birds are safe and will successfully rear a foursome of "noisy plovers."

–July 23, 1987

•

The killdeer is probably the best known plover over most of the U.S. and Canada.

Its brazen, insistent cry of "Killdee! Killdee!" is a for-sure attention getter, for *Charadrius vociferus* is indeed a vociferous bird. Then, too, it claims atten-tion with its boldly marked outfit: two black sashes about the breast, pure white band between the eyes contrasting sharply with the black forehead, as well as a brightly displayed rusty tail with a white rim. These characteristics make it a conspicuous, noisy bird.

And it seems the killdeer is everywhere, apparently a very successful bird at producing many of its own kind from generation to generation.

When I told my grandson Jesse (son of Lyle and Linda Munro Henry) about the Augs-burger killdeer nesting on the ground, he questioned the safety of such a nesting site, saying to me, "But Grandpa, you would think the animals would get them."

Yes, at first it would seem that the ground would be a dan-gerous place to rear a brood of chicks, but it appears to work quite well for the plover.

•

One important part of the kill-deer's lifestyle that perhaps helps the survival record for its eggs and young may be the killdeer's

Killdeer plover feigning injury

remarkable injury-feigning behavior.

Both female and male plovers "guard" the nest by putting on a pitiful act–dragging one wing and squatting on the ground, all the while crying piteously as though in the throes of agony. Many a child (and adult too, for that matter) has been misled by following the "injured" bird, which suddenly, if the pursuer heads away from the nest, recovers and flies away, finally circling back to its eggs or very recently hatched young.

Observers have even seen the killdeer fly up into the face of a grazing cow in a pasture or meadow that has approached too closely for the plover's comfort. Seemingly, this attack often de-

ters the animal, which changes direction, sparing the eggs or young from being trampled.

•

Another ruse of the versatile killdeer is the mock-brooding action. The bird flies and flutters a little distance from the actual site, then suddenly stops and settles down as though squatting on the nest. Again, if approached, the killdeer suddenly loses interest in the mock nest, and may again feign injury, fluttering piteously on broken wings and spreading its tail out fan-like, rusty and shining–an attractive decoy that may lure a pursuing animal away from the nest.

The eggs in the scrape nest are also marvelously well camouflaged, blending in amazingly well with the stones, or cinders and ashen debris, as in the case of the Augsburger plover.

•

In the early 1930s while cultivating sorghum on a farm east of Mentor in Saline County, Kansas, I happened upon a killdeer nest. It was placed on a ridge between the rows and turned out to be an interesting bit of plover craft.

The nest was merely a scrape in the soft soil, but the plovers had decked it out with a "lining" of thin, smooth rock. The shiny flakes were the color of the surrounding bits of reddish, brown, and cream colored stone, mixed in with the clay soil. The chattering plovers extended their ornamentation with what appeared to be a runway laid out with the same type of flat, thin slices of shiny rock.

If you have ever had the opportunity to see killdeer eggs, you can imagine how beautifully the eggs fit the "decor" of the nest and its ornate runway.

—*August 13, 1987*

Retreat for Bird Lovers at Spruce Lake

Is it by your wisdom that the hawk soars,
and spreads his wings toward the south?
Is it at your command that the eagle mounts up
and makes his nest on high?
—Job 39:26-27

In the beautiful Pocono country near Canadensis, Pennsylvania, lies Spruce Lake Camp. Throughout the year many people go to Spruce Lake to attend various retreats that meet the needs and interests of all age groups.

This spring I was privileged to attend a retreat, "For Bird Lovers Only," which has become an annual event at the camp. Again this year, the birds cooperated well. Migrating warblers joined summer and year-round residents to make the retreat an exciting experience.

•

Just prior to the opening of the retreat, Paul Beiler, resident director of Spruce Lake Camp, Leann Kauffman Beiler, and I were sharing birding experiences.

One day Paul and Leann were surprised and delighted when a barred owl plunked itself down on their window feeder. The

Beilers had never before seen such a huge bird patronizing their feeder. Anyway, Paul and Leann used this rare opportunity to photograph a bird that was not expected to drop in, yet for whatever reasons had done so.

Perhaps the owl decided to perch where smaller customers of the window feeder might very handily end up on its own menu. It isn't very likely, however, that the patrons would fall for such an obvious owlish scheme.

·

Another owl-happening seemed rather bizarre for a member of that clan of dignified-looking birds.

Some years ago, John and Elda Waltner Unruh, whose home was tucked away in a delightful woodland near Bluffton, were witnesses to an unusual owl-happening. When they chanced to look out at the birdbath, they could scarcely believe their eyes! There in the birdbath a great horned owl appeared to be blissfully enjoying the bathing facility.

While the huge owl monopolized the bath, no doubt the jays, robins, and other regular patrons of the facility were protesting its outrageous and ludicrous behavior. However, they would take care not to get within reach of the deadly beak and talons of this giant owl that is sometimes fittingly called, "tiger of the air."

Immature barred owl

·

One night of the retreat we attempted to call up a barred owl. Joe and Esther Keeler Pearson played a tape of the calls of this species. In the darkness, the birders waited quietly and expectantly. After a few trials with the taped calls resounding through the dark, wooded area, the answering cry of a barred owl was heard in the distance.

Soon the owl was perched overhead. As Esther manipulated the powerful spotlight, we saw the great bird in the beam. It soon left, then returned. The owl gave us a clear view of its wing pattern as it flew noiselessly out of the clearing and quickly disappeared into the darkness. For all of us, this owl-happening was the high point of the retreat.

·

Just up the slope from the camp reservoir, I saw a redstart busily puttering around what looked like a bunch of moss. When the bird returned a number of times to the site, I realized that it was building a nest about ten feet up in a dead sapling.

Its nest is compactly constructed of plant down, fine grasses, hair, and other material. Some-times the exterior is decorated with lichens and bound together with spider web. The finished nest surely qualifies as the work of an avian artisan of the woodlands.

—July 24, 1980

Church Campers Observe Turtles

O Lord, how manifold are thy works!
In wisdom hast thou made them all;
the earth is full of thy creatures.
            —Psalm 104:24

A few months ago, a stint of March mildness lured this inexperienced midland painted turtle out of the mud in which it had been spending the winter.

Sleepily surveying the situation, the tiny turtle found the weather quite inclement as the brief bit of sunshine disappeared and the temperature dropped.

Soon not even a shadow was cast by the turtle's streamlined body. And what self-respecting turtle, even an immature one, would want to be caught trying to sunbathe when clouds, cold and gray, spread over the March landscape like a soggy, chilly blanket?

Without a backward glance, the disappointed turtle slipped back into the shallows and buried

Young midland painted turtle

itself in the mud at the edge of the pond. But it would soon be back.

•

Chrysemys picta marginata is the beautiful Latin name given our midland painted turtle. Loosely translated, one might say it is a turtle with golden-stitched designs on its marginal scales. The marginals are the small squarish plates along the edge of its upper shell.

This youngster was only about an inch long when it hatched. These infant turtles, as well as the eggs, are eagerly gobbled up by raccoons, muskrats, crows, snakes, other turtles, large fish, and even bullfrogs.

Although a temperature of only 50 degrees has been known to lure painted turtles out of their torpor, a more cozy temperature of 68 degrees is said to be more likely to activate most of our painted turtles. Because at times they burrow down one and one-half feet into the mud, the milder temperatures must last several days before the change reaches the slumbering turtles and triggers responses that bid them hie themselves upward and away to the sunlit logs and beaches of the spring and summer seasons.

•

At Camp Mennoscah in Kingman County, Kansas, the western painted turtle has been found. It and ornate box turtles, softshell turtles, and snapping turtles give campers a good variety to identify.

The docile and beautiful Blanding's turtle can be found at Camp Friedenswald, Cassopolis, Michigan, although they are not numerous. At Friedenswald there has been a history of turtle racing, usually an exciting activity for campers and staff alike.

And yet another species was found in the woods at Camp Men-O-Lan in Pennsylvania. It is the only wood turtle I have ever seen. One source says that the wood turtle makes a very delightful pet. But most of us prefer letting it and the other turtles alone.

Most turtles sold at pet shops die within a few weeks after purchase. Few owners of pet turtles know how to care for them properly. Three turtles that had good care and had grown into large turtles were brought to the pond at the Bluffton Nature Preserve and released. After about a month all were found dead. Apparently they had not learned to fend for themselves in the wild.

•

At Chesley Lake Camp in Lower Ontario, campers had the opportunity to watch a painted turtle covering her eggs. By using only her hind legs, she had dug a pear-shaped hole. Then, after the eggs were laid she threw her legs into reverse, filling the hole. Without ever seeing the eggs, she pushed the loose soil over the eggs, sometimes wetting the soil, causing it to become well packed.

Several years ago a painted turtle made its "nest" alongside the driveway near the garage of Robert and Linda Falk Suter's rural Bluffton home. Since the

Suter's home is close to Riley Creek, I wonder if perhaps some of the turtles we see sunning themselves on logs in the Riley come from that clutch of eggs laid near the Suters' driveway.

—June 25, 1981

Snake River Swirls Through Chasm

Thou makest springs gush forth in the valleys;
they flow between the hills,
...the birds...sing among the branches.
—Psalm 104:10,12

At the invitation of Floyd and Lydia Stutzman Miller, of Meridian, Idaho, I found myself headed for Hell's Canyon in the Rockies as Floyd's guest.

It was early in May, and the gently sloping hills were a sweet green as we climbed northwestward, the basin fading away below us. Having long heard of this fascinating canyon on the border of Idaho and Oregon, I was thrilled to be headed toward it and anticipated the surprises that I knew would await us along the way.

•

Soon we were passing close to Squaw Butte, or so it seemed. Squaw Butte was a landmark that I had first seen from the home of my sister, DeVere (Babe) Ransford, in Meridian, Idaho.

Magpies were prevalent along the way, as were Brewer's blackbirds that are common in the West. Mourning doves and western meadowlarks crossed the highway ahead of us. The liquid, flute-like music of the "field lark of the West" drifted across the foothills, the notes contrasting with the whistled notes of our eastern meadowlark.

The passing scene was fresh, lovely, and peaceful. I enthusiastically anticipated what lay ahead: the mountain valleys, the Snake River, Hell's Canyon.

•

Near Midvale, we stopped to examine some roadside plants bearing bright yellow flowers. It was thrilling to get reacquainted with the heartleaf arnica—I had last seen one 20 years ago across the state in eastern Idaho at the Palisades Mennonite Camp, located in the Targhee National Forest. I was reminded of that campground, its flowering plants, its birds, its campers, and camp leaders. For there I had seen, not

Snake River at Hell's Canyon on the Idaho-Oregon border

only the arnica for the first time, but a similar plant, mules-ears or wyethia, and arrowleaf balsamroot, sego lily, and Indian paintbrush. Beside a tiny stream skirting the camp, yellow monkey flowers, bellflowers, white-flowered watercress, and other plants flourished.

I remembered the beaver our younger campers and I had watched for in that stream as we swatted mosquitoes, and how we had held our breath when the huge, furry engineers surfaced just below us. Even now I thrill at the recollection of the loud splash the beavers made when they slapped their great flat tails on the water after discovering they were being watched.

Yes, seeing the arnica now near Midvale brought back those memories and many more of that earlier time.

•

Hell's Canyon itself cannot be adequately described. The swirling Snake River appears wild, and at places rather furious, as it moves through the 5,500-foot chasm.

Not far from the dam, 20 Canada geese moved near an island in the wide expanse of the Snake River. They appeared to be almost the size of ducks.

At the dam, a pair of kestrels, little falcons, seemed to lack shyness as we watched them there. Perhaps they were young ones, but more probably they had not yet been molested or threatened by visitors to the dam. At one point we approached within a few rods of the pair before they took flight. Then, unexpectedly, they returned to the same site, as we slowly withdrew from the area.

•

On our way home, we made a brief stop at Woodhead Campground near the Brownlee Dam. There I had a pleasant surprise. A fortunate look at a large black bird that flew into a tree near where I was watching some Brewer's blackbirds turned out to be a Lewis's woodpecker.

I had last seen this pink-bellied carpenter 40 years ago while I was serving in a Civilian Public Service camp at Colorado Springs, Colorado. At Brownlee Dam I had but a few moments to check the bird's identity, for the colorful Lewis's woodpecker flew off in its characteristic type of flight, very different from the flight patterns of other woodpeckers.

Perhaps the Lewis's woodpecker was the first exciting bird-find I had experienced after arriving at the CPS camp in 1941. A number of the fly-catching woodpeckers were active there along the sandy stream where great cottonwood trees rattled their waxed leaves above the cool water flowing from the Rocky Mountain foothills.

The sight of a rusty-legged ferruginous hawk helped to put a fitting close to our trip along the Snake River to Hell's Canyon and back.

−May 27, 1982

Prairie, Woodland Along Cedar Creek

The earth brought forth vegetation,
plants yielding seed according to their own kinds,
and trees bearing fruit in which is their seed,
each according to its kind.
And God saw that it was good.
                    −Genesis 1:12

Along Cedar Creek in northeast Indiana, near the town of Leo, is a hilly strip of creekbank where a remnant of prairie and a woodland mingle as a friendly mixed community. In late spring, Kathryn Sauder Moore took her sister, Carolyn Sauder Urich, on a walk through the area. There, socializing easily with prairie plants, were dozens of lovely yellow lady's slippers, whose usual

Large yellow lady's slipper from a hill prairie remnant near Leo, Indiana

home is in shady swamps, wet woods, and edges of bogs. Kathryn counted 90 of the dazzling damsels, then stopped numbering the tribe.

A week later, John and Jackie Sweet Kuehn and I joined Kathryn and Carolyn on a trip to the fascinating site. There we could understand why Kathryn had stopped counting the orchids. They appeared everywhere, nodding their gold-turbaned coiffures in the Indiana sunshine.

John and Jackie were thrilled, for it was their first sighting of the lovely ones, and in such a setting: a *remnant prairie!* It was my third sighting. Never before, however, had I seen more than two in one place. Some 15 years

ago, I unexpectedly came upon a single flowering plant, flourishing on the edge of the marsh at Camp Friedenswald in southern Michigan. Five years later, I found a blossoming pair in West Virginia. But here, along Cedar Creek, they make up a sizable colony. What a thrilling flower-fairyland Kathryn had led us to!

•

Unexpected companions of the lovely orchids were the robust and unrefined but pleasant members of the prairie dock tribe. In their adolescent stage of growth, they appeared coarse but stalwart. Their great leaves, rough and unpliable, could grow to a length of 24 inches, their flower-stalks to a height of 10 feet.

I had brought some from near Bowling Green, Ohio, for our prairie patch. In our plot, they jostle abrasive elbows with several of their cousins, the silphiums and sunflowers, but for them to consort familiarly with orchids seemed a bit incongruous. Yet there they were: lady's slippers and prairie dock sharing a bit of Indiana soil and sun in a most congenial fashion. Such lovely and amiable companions! And we'd like to say, "What an *intentional* community!

•

The orange-yellow puccoon is another pleasant member of a prairie community that rubs gentle shoulders with the orchids from woodland communities.

A racemiferous milkwort contingent seemed at home in the communal settlement. With a fashionable spike of tender buds promising a later floral display, they waited there for a late May parade.

Kathryn later wrote that the milkwort were soon in full bloom, along with red catchfly of shady woodlands, and spiderwort of prairie breeding. She mentions the large baneberries, red cup fungi, wild onion, and wood mint, plus ox-eye daisies abloom in open places—a prelude to the Summer Flower Festival a few weeks later.

•

While prairieland and woodland flowers were on parade during the late spring season, their remnant prairie home was alive with the songs of nonprairie birds.

A yellow-billed cuckoo chucked away in the darker reaches of the woodland. Its retarding yuk-yuks inclined the listeners to feel that the poor "thunder pumper" or "raincrow" was winding down a bit.

An indigo bunting, sounding forth from a perch high in a treetop but screened from our view, hurried through his double-note routine as though he could hardly wait to repeat his favorite number.

Some distance away, in the midst of interesting tree skeletons, a tufted titmouse gave a touch of melancholia to the community, repeating his call in minor key, "Peter! Peter! Peter!" as though in despair of ever locating the wayward Peter.

A spirited cardinal whistled his lively lay from the edge of a field just a cardinal's call away, reminding us of our own hedges and gardens back home. Some of us longed to hear the song of a prairie-loving meadowlark drift over the prairie remnant, as it does where broad expanses of prairie and grasslands strech out beyond unobstructed horizons. That would have made our day.

•

Skirting Cedar Creek on our way back to the car, we were grateful for a refreshing breeze, though it was scarcely boisterous enough to ruffle the wings of the voracious mosquitoes whose presence seemed a bit unprairie-like to us. For we daydreamed of prairies far away, unblemished, ideal, unreal.

Reaching the car, we felt a sincere sense of gratitude to Kathryn Moore for sharing with us something of the beauty and fascination of her hill prairie remnant near Leo, Indiana.

—July 22, 1982

Part III

Summer

Robins Deliver Food, Give Concerts

He causes fountains to flow in the valleys;
...beside them the birds of the heavens dwell,
from among the branches they send forth song.
— Psalm 104:10,12 (Goodspeed)

The mother robin watched the observer closely, cautiously pausing on the cable high above the lawn where she had garnered a beakload of earthworms. Satisfied that all was well, she flew in a roundabout way so that it would be difficult to follow her to the nest.

Waiting for a food delivery, the nestlings had their conveyor systems ready for action the moment food was thrust unceremoniously into their gaping hatches.

Perhaps a hundred times a day, the parents made deliveries to the chicks, amounting to a daily ration of about 200 grams each. During the two weeks as nestlings, the youngsters would consume about three pounds of food. When the young birds were on their own, their parents would start a second and perhaps even a third brood—quite a contribution toward perpetuation of the species.

•

At the Spring Lake Campground at Pandora, Ohio, I watched a robin sitting almost motionless in a tree near Omer and Wanda Lora Gratz's home.

Robin with food for young

It was intriguing to hear the robin lower the volume of his song to produce a whisper-like quality very pleasant to my ear and evidently to his also. At intervals he would sing the first few *chir-rups* at a rather normal volume, followed by the introspective, subdued rendition. I gained the impression that he was more than a bit enchanted by his own performance. Perhaps he awarded it a most excellent rating while arbitrarily giving an average score to the more orthodox robins in his neighborhood.

No doubt his mate was nearby and was flattered by the efforts of the avian virtuoso whom she probably believed was performing solely for her enjoyment–and perhaps he was.

•

An observer at the LL & J Ranch in Pemberville, Ohio, noted that a particular robin always faced the same direction while engaged in concert from his favorite perch. Later it was discovered that the song was echoed back to the gifted performer from a cluster of farm buildings close by.

Perhaps like Narcissus, who was enamored by his own image in a pool, the vain avian artist had become infatuated with his own voice. But that was probably better than to have mistaken the echoes for voices of rivals. In that case, like Don Quixote of old, he might have foolishly sallied forth to do battle with imaginary challengers staring at him from windows of the farmyard buildings.

I once observed a modern robin Don Quixote challenging a wire fence in our yard. Its beak already loaded with straws, the ambitious thrush added a length of twine that was attached to the fence. When he attempted to move on, the fence refused to release the twine. Dropping the straw, he took a firm grip on the twine, braced himself and gave a hefty heave-to (usually a very effective procedure when dealing with an earthworm). Still the fence gave no quarter. The robin tried to ignore the opposition by flying off with the string, but he was jerked back. He tried the tactic a second time, but the shock sent him to the fencetop to ponder the problem.

A few moments of robin reflection must have convinced him that the string wasn't worth fighting for, so he went back to gathering straw for his nest in the sugarpear tree. Perhaps he rationalized his defeat by repeating the proverb, "Discretion is the better part of valor." And perhaps it is.

•

A lusty robin once set up an observation post near the home of our neighbors, Joe Jr. and Carolyn Sauder Urich. The bird sang as though its very life depended on it. The robin's almost frenetic *chir-upping* sometimes continued without interruption for about an hour in the morning and another in the evening.

The robin probably had a very definite territory staked out and no doubt other robins in the neighborhood were fully aware of the dangers involved in infringing on that claim. Just what triggered its excessive outbursts may be a mystery to us, but it was no doubt very reasonable to members of the robin clan who could ask many questions about our behavior as they sit in the maples and engage in people-watching.

—*July 12, 1979*

Historic Mollet's Quarry site on Big Riley Creek, Bluffton, Ohio

A Boat Trip on Big Riley Creek

And God saw everything that he had made, and behold, it was very good.
—Genesis 1:31

A little two-seated boat, assembled and made sea worthy by Herman Hilty of rural Bluffton, silently drifted along with the current of Big Riley Creek. Only a nudge or two from a paddle was needed to avoid the boulders that stubbornly braced their smooth, granite shoulders against the water of the creek—a patient adversary which drummed them with wave after persistent wave.

Soon a pair of flapping wings with blue patches lifted a reluctant teal from the shadows where the colorful drake had been idly dabbling in the gentle eddies along the north bank.

Disturbed while sun bathing, several painted turtles slipped noiselessly into cool water, while a drowsy yellowhammer lightly tapped out a lazy tattoo in the cottonwood overhead.

In routine fashion, a cruising crow reported its position somewhere in the distance. No acknowledgment was heard from the clan's lone flight controller perched high in the cottonwood.

•

From overhanging branches, eastern kingbirds darted forth in self-confident sallies, pursuing flying insects drawn to the stream by forces unknown to the observers.

I recalled my boyhood in Kansas when we children released moths (we called them "millers") to be snatched up by both the eastern and the western kingbirds. The two species of "bee martins," as we sometimes called the kingbirds, were often seen perched on the barbed wire fences in apparent harmony. I remembered when a scissor-tailed flycatcher with its pink-tinted wing linings and sides, was first seen by members of our family as it tugged at a red ribbon held fast to the clothesline by an old fashioned clothespin.

Farther along the Big Riley, a relative of the kingbirds, the alder or Traill's flycatcher, called out *fits-bew*, the Ohio version of the species' song. In other states they call *wee-BE-o*, or another variation. I first heard this version in a marsh at Camp Amigo near Sturgis, Michigan. Last year, Denny Weaver and Harvey Hiebert heard a number of these tiny flycatchers along the Riley in July, suggesting that they probably nest here. (Since this was written, the birds giving the two different calls have been separated into two species, the willow flycatcher and the alder flycatcher.)

The mellow call of a rose-breasted grosbeak came from close to the creek. Finally it was in full view—a real thrill to Herman who never before had the privilege of hearing and seeing this beautiful bird.

•

We saw a common water snake swimming near the left bank of the creek. I first identified this snake some years ago at Camp Mennoscah in Kansas. It had been fishing near the plank dam in the Ninnescah River. As the snake swam away with a minnow held crosswise in its mouth, it held its prey above the water, much like a water spaniel fetches its catch to its master.

We finally entered deep water at the historical Mollet Quarry that has been out of operation for many years. Earlier, Herman used to sit next to a limestone face in the quarry as water cascaded over him on its way downstream. Only a remnant of that barrier remains to mark the spot where limestone blocks were once cut and removed from their ancient bed.

•

A delightful surprise was ours when suddenly a flotilla of young pied-billed grebes went spattering ahead of us, their feet barely touching the water as they fled downstream. We saw an adult dive, as the youngsters must have done later, for when we next saw them, they were swimming along the opposite bank. As we were getting ready to disembark, they entered a channel on the other side, perhaps startling the muskrat engaged in carrying vegetation to its burrow. So ended a pleasant boat trip on Big Riley Creek.

—June 28, 1979

Birds and Blossoms in New England

Remember the wonderful works that he has done,
his miracles, and the judgments he uttered.
—Psalm 105:5

These tree swallows parked on a sign on Plum Island in northeastern Massachusetts can survey the surrounding area for flying insects.

Dozens of bird boxes placed over the area offer free tenancy for any swallow desiring housing in the vicinity. Of course, they are expected to help keep the area as free from insects as possible so that the benefits will work both for the tenants and for human visitors to the island.

In addition to the Hellcat Swamp Nature Trail, Plum Island is enhanced by Parker River Wildlife Refuge. There, over 300

Tree swallows on Plum Island

species of birds have been tallied. Black ducks, greater scaup ducks, Canada geese, and many shorebirds find sanctuary there where sand dunes, salt and fresh water marshes, tidal waters, and a glacial upland area join to make Plum Island an intriguing place to roam.

•

On our visit to New England, I had the privilege of seeing a flock of about 20 glossy ibis in a marsh on Plum Island. It was my first sighting of the beautiful bronze-chestnut marsh bird and a delightful surprise because I did not expect to find them that far north. The Peabody Museum of Salem has one mounted specimen which they noted was a rare bird in Massachusetts. To me, the fact that the range of the glossy ibis is gradually extending farther north is a pleasing development.

I also saw black-crowned night herons on the island along with a lone swan whose mate might have been incubating on a nest hidden in the area. We were told, however, of a particular swan that was known to approach visitors for a handout. At any rate, this one was far out in the marsh, apparently seeking its own board in the tradition of generations of untamed, industrious members of the swan tribe.

•

Along a trail in the Ipswich River Sanctuary near Topsfield, a tiny pool snuggles in the lap of the surrounding area. From a rustic bench I could hear the distant crowing of a cock pheasant. Later, the presence of a crow in flight was announced with a surprisingly casual pronouncement. This quiet call would indicate that, when circumstances demand it, even the usually raucous crow can communicate in a contented manner to inform family and friends of its flight position and that all is well.

On a small log along the west bank, two painted turtles were absorbing filtered sunlight in an atmosphere of pastoral tranquility. Later they slipped easily into the water's edge where fawn lilies were in bloom.

The quiet serenity of the scene was punctuated at intervals by the chipping of a chipmunk. Like the contented crow, perhaps Chippy was keeping his kinfolk aware of where its garnering chores were being carried on.

At Essex, the largest scillas I had ever seen were in bloom at Charles and Marty Drake's home where I was a guest. I don't know whether or not the scillas were of a special stock, but they were about twice as tall as the largest ones in our Ohio garden.

Seeing the great black-backed gull, the largest species of gulls in the United States, was another special experience for me as we visited the fisherman's wharf at Gloucester. These giant gulls, sometimes called "saddle-backed" gulls, are resident from Arctic areas to Long Island, New York, having extended their southward range in the past few decades. Seeing the great black-backed gulls helped bring my brief visit to the Bay State in historic New England to an exciting climax.

—June 29, 1978

A young raccoon

The Raccoon: Masked Night Raider

He sends the night and darkness, when all the forest folk come out.
—Psalm 104:20 (Living Bible)

Pah-su-de'na is the euphonious name given the raccoon by the Taos Indians of southwest United States.

One summer while camping in Palo Duro Canyon near Amarillo, Texas, I suspected nightly visits by the attractive prowler. One evening I set up a crude alarm system of tent poles and skillets. Suddenly during the stillness of the night, the din of clanging metal awakened me. From my tent I beheld the largest, fattest raccoon I had ever seen.

The din had not awakened the golden-fronted woodpeckers, scaled quails, canyon wrens, road-runners, and other inhabitants of this isolated canyon in the Texas Panhandle. But while they slept, the portly *Pa-su-de'na* waddled away to seek a quieter dining area, as the clean sand beneath the shallow ripples of Palo Duro Creek glistened and sparkled under an expansive Texas moon.

•

Raccoons are likely to visit campgrounds at any season of the year. Half-starved, mangy-looking raccoons ran amok in a campground at Georgia's Oke-fenokee National Wildlife Refuge one winter when Maurice Kaufmann and I camped there with some Bluffton College students in mid-January.

At suppertime, even before nightfall, the raccoons fairly swarmed over our benches and tables in a desperate search for food. Some were badly scarred, others had open wounds, in-curred, perhaps, in fierce com-petition for the lean pickings left by the few campers frequenting the area during the winter season.

In the nearby swamplands, alligators, otters, herons, ibises, and other native fishers of Okefenokee country continued their individual, independent life-styles. But even with natural food available, these "tame" rac-coons, made dependent on con-tinuous handouts by well-meaning campers, had degenerated into pitiful "bums"—hardly recogniz-able as part of a clan whose members are known as attractive, skilled citizens of the wildlife community.

•

Once while I was birding in the countryside near Goessel, Kansas, I found nesting green herons to be surprisingly common, even along small streams bordered by scattered trees.

Near a small creek I stumbled onto a trash pile almost over-grown with vegetation. The after-noon sun shone on what ap-peared to be a mass of brown-ish-gray hair inside an old nail keg. I casually kicked the keg. To my surprise, a startled raccoon, disturbed from his siesta, scram-bled from his cozy pad and beat a blinking, blundering retreat into the brush.

Perhaps he sought a safer site in which to relax after working the nightshift. During the day-shift, a large crew of herons em-ployed patience and skill as they spear-fished for minnows, frogs, and crayfish. It seemed like unfair competition to poor *Pro-cyon lotor* who was limited to hand-fishing and had to wear a pair of black goggles.

•

A midnight raid took place one summer night when members of the Girls' Club of the First Mennonite Church of Wadsworth, Ohio, camped at Mohican State Park.

When most of the campers were asleep, a dashing band of masked night-raiders suddenly and unceremoniously descended on the camp. Swinging lids of trash cans clanged and clattered, while the sound of raiders crashing through the underbrush made it appear that two score and ten brigands were overrunning the premises.

Suddenly the band of raccoons disappeared into the night. For the few campers who had been awake, it was an interesting and exciting experience. No real harm was done, but the bits of scattered trash indicated that the gang had never learned to execute a nice, clean raid that would have distinguished them as a well-disciplined troop of clever and mischievous looters.

•

"Help! Help! Would someone please help!" A woman's cry broke the nighttime stillness of a campground at the Pinery Provincial Park, in Grand Bend, Ontario.

Awakened by the call, a camper ran with flashlight and located two women and a small boy standing by their tent. "We had no flashlight, and we heard a bear or something in the bushes!" they said.

An open bag of marshmallows lay on the ground. The camper assured them that there were no bears in the park, but that raccoons sometimes make a lot of noise. Noting the visitor's nightclothes, one apologized, "Oh, we didn't mean to wake you!" A possible response: "That's okay. I usually run around the park in my nightclothes at three o'clock in the morning."

Back in the tent, this sandy footed camper, though a bit amused, thought it a pity the little lad could not have seen a real, live, wild raccoon munching on a marshmallow. Perhaps the little boy also liked "raw" marshmallows, especially if he had to wait too long for a toasted one.

—October 20, 1977

Nighthawks and their Relatives

May the glory of the Lord endure for ever,
may the Lord rejoice in his works....
　　　　　　　　　　—Psalm 104:31

This young nighthawk might have been hatched from a make-shift nest on a flat roof amid the noise of city traffic. These birds have adapted well to the changes made by humans. Some use the graveled roofs in the cities for nesting sites.

When perched in trees, nighthawks are very difficult to see. They usually rest horizontally on a branch, the mottled feathers camouflaging them very efficiently. This camouflage worked well when Dwight Platt of Newton, Kansas, and I were lucky to spot one perched on a light gray branch of a cottonwood near Harvey County Park some years ago.

•

The chuck-will's-widow is a large relative of the nighthawk. Dwight and I once saw one in western Harvey County, Kansas, where the Sand Prairie Natural History Reservation is now located. We noticed the bird resting on the sandy ground before it flew off with its characteristic moth-like flight.

In a list of the birds of Harvey County, Kansas, compiled by Edna L. Ruth, Alma Ruth, and Ruth Rose, the chuck-will's-

Young nighthawk

widow is reported as an uncommon May migrant.

At Thompkin's Bayou near Gulfport, Mississippi, I had my first encounter with the chuck-will's-widow's characteristic call. It took a while before I realized it was accenting the wrong syllable for a nighthawk. So while the day campers were busy pulling blue crabs from the bayou, I was engrossed in listening to a bird who kept himself out of sight while making his presence known by his vocalizing.

The chuck-will's-widow, often called the bull bat, is a common summer resident at Pine Lake Camp near Meridian, Mississippi. Every night for about two weeks each summer, the bull bats keep up a continuous session of the loud calls. When I was there, the birds sounded forth even after midnight, until campers and staff went to sleep with the calls still ringing in their ears.

Until the last night of camp, neither campers nor staff saw a single Chuck-will's-widow, although their calls were prevalent. That night several of them flew over us just after dark during a campfire service, and we finally caught a glimpse of the birds that had intrigued us by their nightly vocal performances.

•

The poor-will is another member of this large-mouthed, insectivorous tribe. Although generally more western in distribution, some are found in the South. Maurice Kaufmann and I saw one as we traveled along a highway in the Everglades National Park in Florida, its eyes glowing red in the headlights of our automobile.

At the Palisades Mennonite camp in Idaho, we often heard the poor-will call from the ridge above camp in the Targhee National Forest. One evening as we were ascending the trail toward camp, a poor-will flew ahead of us and sat there until we approached too closely. It then took off and repeated the performance as though it greatly enjoyed people-watching.

•

One summer morning on the Tilmar and Evelyn Schrock Kaufman farm near Moundridge, Kansas, the familiar call of a whip-poor-will sounded forth loud and clear. This seemed strange, for I had never heard one in the area.

Upon investigation, the call appeared to be coming from the top of the silo. A strange place for a whip-poor-will, I thought, and besides, the morning was not the most likely time for a whip-poor-will happening. The suspicions were valid, for there on the top-most rung of the silo sat a mockingbird, whipping poor Will in a very convincing manner.

Perhaps the delightful mimic had picked up the call while wintering farther south. Now he was enthusiastically using it in his routine as though this newly acquired addition to its repertoire especially suited its fancy. And besides, if the mocker had a sense of humor it must have had a chuckle from fooling at least one member of its audience.

–July 14, 1977

Countryside scene near Dayton, Tennessee

New Friends in Sunny Tennessee

...let the field exult, and everything in it!
    —Psalm 96:12a

It was midafternoon when Cindy Lehman, formerly of Kidron, Ohio, and now living at Meridian, Mississippi, and I arrived at the home of the Merlin and Mary Brenneman Grieser family on the edge of Dayton, Tennessee. Soon the Grieser children, three-year-old Michael and five-year-old Myra, were bringing us tiny fistfulls of flowers and other plants.

Later they brought us some especially colorful blossoms from plants known as Venus's looking glass. *Triodanis perfoliata* bears attractive violet-blue flowers tucked in the axils of leaves that clasp the stem. The flowers secrete nectar that is attractive to bumblebees, smaller wild bees, several kinds of small flies, and some butterflies.

The children never seemed to tire of making trip after trip to the field, returning with various kinds of offerings from the uncultivated plot.

•

As the late afternoon wore on, the almost cloying fragrance of Japanese honeysuckle settled around us while we visited on the lawn. We stayed out to enjoy the beautiful evening. Once in a while, the call of a bobwhite reached us from somewhere near the western border of the field. The clear, flute-like whistle of a meadowlark added to the musical background, while the state bird of Tennessee, the mockingbird, went through its varied routine from a thicket along the distant fence line.

Overhead, chimney swifts expertly darted in pursuit of flying insects, while a black-masked yellowthroat added a bit of mystery as it sounded out an emphatic "witchery-witchery-witchery" from its territory, probably in the vicinity of a marsh or other wet area.

At dusk we were pleased to hear the distinct lashing call of a whip-poor-will. Its wide mouth would serve it well as a trap for large insects as it dived and swooped, garnering its prey with apparent ease and finesse.

A rooster, probably from some neighboring farmyard, did not wait for morning to declare its presence and importance to the other members of the chicken clan. No doubt they were duly impressed by chanticleer's cocky challenge.

•

Ten days later, on my way back to Ohio from Alabama, I again had the privilege of being a guest of the Grieser family.

It was interesting to note how those few days had affected the vegetation in the field and garden. The plants had not only grown in height, but several new ones were in full blossom.

An interesting plant then in flower was the sleepy catchfly. It has an inflated bladder just below its very small petals. The stem often secretes a sticky fluid in which small insects are sometimes caught. The "sleepy" part of the common name results from the tendency of the flowers to close under cloudy skies or when carried into the house.

•

The Grieser garden had also matured a lot during those ten days. Tender head lettuce was in prime condition for the table. String beans would soon be ready for snapping. Potatoes were of ample size to tempt the cook to dig a few in order to serve the popular combination of new potatoes and green peas.

As I left for Ohio the next day, the fragrance of honeysuckle was again in the air and the mockingbird called from a hedge. These sensations and many other delightful experiences would be etched in my memory as a part of a brief visit with new friends in sunny Tennessee.

–July 13, 1978

Mourning dove at the Karl and Ada Steiner Gierman home, Bluffton, Ohio

Mourning Dove Builds Slipshod Nest

For lo, the winter is past... The flowers appear on the earth.
The time of singing has come, and the voice of the turtledove
is heard in our land.

—Song of Solomon 2:11-12

At Karl and Ada Steiner Gierman's home, a pair of mourning doves and their young refused to relinquish their claim to a spruce scheduled to be removed to make way for construction of a garage.

Finally the young were on their own. The Giermans could proceed with their building plans without worrying about the tenacious squatters that for a time, at least, had sole and uncontested possession of the nesting site. We give credit to these birds for being so resolute–a trait admired by most of us. We also commend Karl and Ada for their consideration in leaving the doves undisturbed until the young left the nest.

•

If any bird in our area is a slob at nest building, it is the mourning dove, *Zenaida macroura*.

Now, I'm not faulting the bird for trying to avoid blistering its soft beak by toting loads of building material, nor would I have it waste its time trying to put up a fancy shanty that will only be used for a scant four weeks. However, when it comes to how their nests look, these happy-go-lucky *palomas* just seem to have no pride–that lovely virtue that helped make our country great.

For instance, this is their method (if one can call it a method) for constructing their avian home-sweet-home: a few unchoice twigs are tossed haphazardly crosswise, but if they are to drop lengthwise, that seems to be okay, too. Hardly anything resembling a lining is laid in the nest, and often you may look up through the rickety platform and gaze on the bonnie blue sky above.

This being the case, it is little wonder that often an egg or two will drop through the cracks and break on the ground below. And during a rainstorm, my what a pity! Many are the nestlings blown out of the makeshift nests to die of exposure. For sure, the building code for dove nests is not enforced or else does not exist in dovian society.

•

But then, perhaps the bird is partly justified for building a slipshod nest, for reportedly, the female does much of the work.

Maybe she just figures that if she does most of the construction and engineering, single-handedly laying out the twigs as well as laying the eggs, while her spouse sits around moaning to himself, then why should she spend her precious time trying to slap together a nifty nest.

With that in mind we can sort of sympathize with her. After all, she cannot be doing too punk a job, for look at the flocks of doves that greatly outnumber many of our other bird species.

•

Even though we make fun of their nest construction, those peaceful birds have some family traits that we homebodies admire and even wish our fellow citizens would emulate.

Both papa and mama mourning dove share in incubation duties. Papa takes the day shift while the lady of the house takes over in the evening. Surely that is a commendable bit of connubial cooperation every modern and enlightened citizen will applaud.

One gentle evening in the merry month of May, I climbed a ladder to photograph a faithful female engaged in her dovian duty on a nest in our Norway spruce. A second dove was perched just above the nest; that one, I thought, must be the male who has just been relieved by his mate. So I took my own sweet time to position myself for the photograph I hoped to take.

Suddenly the dove above the nest descended and sidled onto the eggs, while the mate on the nest moved over and flew chuckling out of the tree. Not for a moment were the eggs left uncovered. But I, taken by surprise, just stood there with my mouth open. Imagine! I, a member of that supposedly most intelligent group of superior beings, *Homo sapiens*, had just been shown up by a duo of what I thought were just dumb doves!

•

I had missed a rare opportunity to photograph the "changing of the guard." Yes, I blew it! Oh well, the picture probably would not have turned out so well anyway!

—*March 25, 1988*

The Life and Times of Heecliff the Dove

I know all the birds of the air,
and all that moves in the field is mine.
—Psalm 50:11

Some years ago when Roger and Cathy Snider Siebert were living in Pandora, they called me to report that a white dove was perched in their garage. When I arrived at their house, I offered some feed to the dove, which accepted a bit from my outstretched hand. The Sieberts offered to let me take the bird with me to identify it and perhaps return it to its owner. So I captured the dove and put it in my car for the drive home.

When I parked in downtown Pandora, I happened to stop by an auto whose driver was Thom McDonald of the nearby town of Gilboa. Thom quickly identified the bird as a Java dove. This species is often used by magicians who are adept at pulling white doves from black hats and other such unlikely containers. Thom can pull a number of such tricks himself, and he instantly recognized the dove as soon as he saw the bird in my car.

•

Javana, as we temporarily called the dove, was later adopted by our son, Larry, who took it to share his Alley View apartment in nearby Ottawa.

Larry soon renamed the dove Heecliff. Perhaps because he had tasted sweet freedom for a while before he was captured and again

Afghan, offspring of Heecliff and Gertrude

placed in a cage, Heecliff fussed and fretted in his small home. Feeling sorry for the bird, Larry often released the Java dove, permitting him to roam the apartment. But Heecliff, confusing liberty with license, went merrily about, stripping some of Larry's favorite houseplants until they were mere skeletons of their former selves. To make matters even worse, Heecliff would fly from his mischievous doings, laughing (or so it seemed to Larry) as he fled. Such goings-on became quite a problem until two of Larry's friends stepped in to alleviate the worsening situation.

As a Christmas present, the friends contributed a grand cage, ample enough at least to help Heeclif endure living in his new deluxe apartment for longer periods before becoming stir crazy.

Again Heecliff would be freed for short periods of time. He seemed to be under less stress now that he had a larger cage in which to work off his excess energy. Soon some of the larger plants began to recover from Heecliff's maulings. Others, however, had to be replaced.

•

Sometimes when released, Heecliff would fly to the washer where he would stand and coo, bow, and otherwise divert himself as he saw his reflection in the stainless steel of the instrument panel. This gave Larry an idea: How would Heecliff's restlessness be affected if a mate could be found for him? This idea was soon implemented when Jim Smeltzer from Gilboa loaned Larry a ringed turtle dove to keep Heecliff company. Neither Jim nor Larry knew if the new companion was a lady dove; they hoped Gertrude, as Larry called it, was a lady bird. They were soon to find out.

One day Larry noticed that both Heecliff and Gertrude were acting strangely–both sitting quietly on their perches, not busily moving around as was their custom. Larry, inexperienced in knowing what to do for a possibly expectant dove mother, hastily put a rag into the cage. Later when he returned from work at the LK Restaurant, sure enough, a pearly-white egg, as pretty as you please, was sitting on the cloth. For sure now, Gertrude was a lady!

•

Later, two glossy eggs were incubated in the manner of a mourning dove: Heecliff sat on the eggs during the day; Gertrude took over at night. Finally, after about 16 days, two homely baby doves hatched, apparently consisting of nothing but beak and differential.

Larry immediately named them Afghan and Stan. From the start, Stan didn't fare very well, and soon he died. Afghan thrived though and quickly became a tame and lovable adolescent. Gertrude, unlike her mate Heecliff, remained rather wild. Heecliff was as mischievous as before, and just as likable. Sometimes, it seems, parenthood doesn't change the parents one bit!

•

Postlude: With Afghan in the cage, three *palomas* became a crowd. So Afghan was sold. Gertrude, the untamed one, disappeared one day when she and Heecliff were released to perch in the trees growing in the yard of the place in Ottawa where Larry, his wife Virginia Basinger, and their son Will lived. The aging Heecliff fell victim to a roving pussy cat one day when enjoying his daily release from his cage. Thus concluded the era that began with Heecliff, the snow-white Java dove, and ended with a situation that no magician could control, even with the most skillful sleight-of-hand magic.

–January 12, 1989

Plants and Animals in an Ontario Park

He has made everything beautiful in its time.
—Ecclesiastes 3:11

With its pink floral heads softly etched against the sky, the cylindric blazing star, *Liatris cylindracea*, seems right at home among the sand dunes of the Pinery Provincial Park, Grand Bend, Ontario.

The blazing stars or gayfeathers are among the most spectacular flowering plants of midsummer to early autumn in areas of central and eastern North America suitable to their growth.

Before western settlement the plains Indians boiled *Liatris* leaves and corms to obtain a decoction for treatment of diarrhea in their children. For most of us, however, the beauty of their fresh blossoms and dried spikes for winter bouquets is reason enough to appreciate them in meadow and garden.

The Pinery Provincial Park has three species of blazing star (*L. aspera, cylindracea, and spicata*) that have their special niches in the park. For example, the dense blazing star, *L. spicata*, grows best in the more moist parts of the park. The tall slender stalks with their dense floral spikes remind me of giant editions of the sparklers used in our Fourth of July celebrations.

Cylindric blazing star

•

This summer we passed a number of the dense blazing stars in the low, moist areas before we ascended the dunes in search for the ant lion pits we knew were in the area. Higher up among the cylindric blazing stars we found a number of the tiny pits under a sandy ledge. At the bottom of each cone-shaped trap, an ant lion patiently waited for some small insect to stumble into the pit and slide to the bottom.

One time we found a pit close to an ant colony. Perhaps it was happenstance, but maybe an un-usually wily ant lion had purpose-fully selected a site where the living was easy. And no one but an ant could fault him for that.

•

A fidgety eastern chipmunk was a frequent and welcome visitor to our campsite at the riverside campground.

From somewhere among the aromatic sumac, woodland sun-flowers, wild bergamot, and flowering spurge of the area, Chippy often ventured forth from his secret den in search of food.

Our eleven-year-old daughter, Mona, was constantly entertained by the little beastie, luring him closer and closer by well-spaced kernels of popcorn. Finally the nervous but nervy free-loader ate out of Mona's hand. By actual count, the enterprising chipmunk toted a total of at least 40 kernels of popcorn in his cheek pouches at one haul. At that rate his den should soon be amply stocked for winter.

•

A jet-black squirrel, a race of the gray squirrel, was perched on a table at a neighboring campsite. It was seriously munching on sunflower seeds left by previous campers for just such visitors that might drop in for a snack.

One summer while camping at the Pinery, we saw a black squirrel stretched out on a shaded branch, his legs limp and dangling. Probably this was his way of staying cool, as a slight breeze wafted his lazy limbs and tousled tail, providing welcome air conditioning on a hot August day.

•

From our campsite, we heard the call of a whip-poor-will every night. When Iva Caddick and Mahlon and Marie Zehr Leis from Tavistock stopped to visit us at our campsite, Iva told us that she had heard the call of the whip-poor-will, as well as another simi-lar call, while in Florida. Accord-ing to her description the other cry must have been that of a chuck-will's-widow, a common summer resident of that state.

•

In addition to the area birds, other wildlife came to our camp-site. The visitors included an American toad and some raccoons. The latter made nightly forays, hoping to find delicacies that they could enjoy while the campers were fast asleep in their tents.

—*September 8, 1977*

Ingenious Toads Feast on Insects

*And God said, "Let the earth bring forth
every kind of animal...
and wildlife of every kind."
And so it was.*
—Genesis 1:24 (Living Bible)

This western toad is walking or crawling, although it can also hop. Crawling is a trait of the true toads, whose generic title is *Bufo*, probably coming from the same root as "buffoon," which denotes a clown or jester. A good look at the face of a toad does tend to make us think the title is an appropriate one.

Arnold and Melva Kane Ewy found this California version of the common garden toad, *Bufo boreas,* at their home near Reedley. Whether walking or hopping, *Bufo boreas* gets to where the insects are all year long. In California, even during the month of January, he demonstrated that, though he may look like a buffoon, he manages to capture enough insects to survive without handouts from anybody. In these days of inflation, that is no mean accomplishment.

•

Once, Betty Bixel Heiks of rural Bluffton noticed a toad nestled in a cozy hollow at the base of an old stump near her home. Soon she observed that, though the toad was never seen outside its niche, as the

Western toad from Reedley, California

weeks rolled by it seemed to be growing larger. But how could it grow without leaving its snug apartment?

Later she noted that carpenter ants and other insects were plentiful in and around the stump. Evidently *Bufo americanus* solved its food problem by letting its insect visitors deliver themselves to its door where they were lapped up without ceremony and at no charge to the ingenious toad.

It is no wonder that the toad appeared to be grinning widely. With no grocery bills nor delivery costs to pay, who wouldn't wear a smile even at the risk of being called a comical buffoon!

•

The great plains toad lets it presence be known in an unmistakable manner when conditions are ideal for its chorus to engage in concert.

Once when my son Larry and I were walking along the terraces on Tilmar and Evelyn Schrock Kaufman's farm near Moundridge, Kansas, the *Bufo cognatus* chorus was executing what we considered to be a deafening performance not especially suited to our musical taste. Although it is poor manners to shout while a great musical is being rendered, Larry and I resorted to just such poor decorum as we tried to converse. Our rude manners seemed not to bother the chorus members one whit. They energetically continued to perform what was no doubt a flawless rendition of an ageless repertoire; one that was probably forever new and exciting to the batrachian kinfolk for whom it was sung.

Looking back at the incident it is a pity that Larry and I had not listened with more respect and appreciation to what must have been a concert steeped in the ancient toadlore of a venerable race.

•

The spadefoot is an interesting toad that has a sharp-edged "spade" on each hind foot, and pupils that are vertical in bright light.

During a rainy spell in Kansas, a chorus of spadefoot toads was performing in a shallow pool back of Carnegie Hall, a building formerly on the Bethel College campus. After but a few weeks they disappeared along with the temporary pools from which they had sung.

A few years later, on his farm near Burrton, Kansas, Joe Schrag found some toads buried deep in the soil where he was laying out an irrigation system. We can only guess that they might have been spadefoot toads, for *Scaphiopus bombifrons* is marvelously equipped to excavate such deep underground hideaways.

—May 11, 1978

Nature's intriguing design: a skeletonized leaf

Some Birds Hitchhike on Others' Backs

Great is our Lord, and abundant in power;
his understanding is beyond measure.
*   —Psalm 147:5*

While on a nature walk at the Bluffton College Nature Preserve, Jason Barborak, a third grader from Brenda Geiger's class, brought me this skeletonized leaf that he found on the ground near the college cabin. For some time I had been on the lookout for one of these natural objects, because I liked the pattern which, as you can see, exhibits a netted or reticulated design, which reminds me of a piece of old lace.

The above photo shows a network formed by the veins of a leaf–in this case a leaflet from a compound leaf of the shagbark hickory. This particular leaflet was probably one of the three upper leaflets, because the other two at the base of the compound leaf are usually smaller and have a slightly different form.

The softer parts of the leaflet have been broken down by bacteria and minute insects that use the material as food.

The leaf had fallen to the ground where it came in contact with moisture in a soil rich in microscopic organisms. The result is an interesting and lovely design—another example of nature's art work.

•

One of the highpoints of the wayside revelations of this past year was an experience I had while hiking at the Florissant Fossil Beds Natural Monument near Divide, Colorado.

Don Troyer of the Rocky Mountain Mennonite Camp took myself and two others to examine an area of ponderosa pine that showed evidence of bark removal by Native Americans who had lived in the area long ago. The park naturalist told us that a golden eagle had a nest in one of the pines bordering a high ridge of rocks not far from the fossil beds.

On the way to the historic pines, we spotted an eagle soaring in the vicinity. On the return walk, several of us with binoculars watched an eagle being pestered by a bird which we presumed was a red-winged blackbird. The small bird suddenly dropped, appearing to land on the back of the huge eagle. After at least five seconds of apparent hitchhiking, the small bird again took to the air on his own power and disappeared into the wild blue yonder.

Another member of our party saw and concluded the same thing without the aid of binoculars. A hiker we met farther up the trail observed the same activity.

It was my first acquaintance with this kind of occurrence, but no doubt other bird watchers have witnessed the same piggyback behavior of smaller birds riding the backs of eagles and perhaps other large birds.

Centuries ago, we are told, people believed that smaller birds hitched rides across the Mediterranean on the backs of large birds such as eagles and kites. Now it is easier for me to understand those stories, for others have observed similar instances. So perhaps such hitchhiking episodes aren't that bizarre after all.

—January 14, 1988

Pine Lake, Meridian, Mississippi

Observing the Denizens of Pine Lake

Let the heavens be glad, and let the earth rejoice...
Then shall all the trees of the wood sing for joy....
*—*Psalm 96:11-12

Pine Lake, as its name indicates, has many pines gracing its shores. At the Pine Lake Mennonite Camp, Camp Director Orlo Kaufman and I, together with other campers, explored the area.

A variety of flowering plants flourish near the lake. Using a wildflower guidebook, we identified a few plants new to us.

An attractive beauty, candy root, *Polygala nana*, bears a short but bright tuft of orange-yellow blossoms. Its root has an aroma of wintergreen, containing what is known in pharmacy as *senega*. American Indians and early settlers used it as an antidote for the bites of poisonous snakes.

As we neared the west end of the lake, a green heron, interested in frogs and fishes more than in flowers, squawked as it took off for a more secluded spot in which to use its spearfishing skills without interference from flower fanciers.

•

Near the lake, a charming little legume, the pencil flower, *Stylo-*

santhes biflors, flaunted a single, conspicuous blossom to passing admirers.

North of the lake, a colony of spectacular Indian pinks, *Spigelia marilandica*, sporting curved racemes of red-petaled blossoms lined with yellow, brightened a somber spot in the moist, shady woods.

Along the southern shore, we found an eastern mud turtle in a shallow channel easing into the lake. We soon released it to do whatever it was in the process of doing when rudely interrupted by an inquisitive visitor to the lake marsh community.

Camper Ted Selig spotted an armadillo as we explored the woods above the lake. Tearing after the animal like a do-or-die zealot, Ted tripped over stones and brambles. Although the short-legged mammal apparently was no match for the long-legged biped, it had an escape route planned for just such an emergency. Quickly the wily beast low-tailed it into its den, which was artfully concealed by stone and brush.

I had barely missed a coveted photo subject, but I rationalized that up north, some might dismiss the photo as a picture of extinct creatures from the age of dinosaurs in a museum exhibit.

•

Soon after sunset, the lake began to take on a different aspect as voices of the night slowly started to sound off, singly or in chorus.

The bronze frog's first banjo-like twang signalled others to follow suit. Somehow, at first, they seemed unwilling or unable to perform in concert. The effect, however, was exciting, as various individuals seemingly modified their pitch just enough to bring out many nuances of tone. As I listened, I was reminded of a string ensemble tuning up before a concert.

At intervals, the husky bull-frog's deep, resonant bass added a pleasing dimension to the carnival of sound. Meanwhile, dozens of tiny cricket frogs joined in. Their voices, resembling the clicking together of two small pebbles, contributed a low-keyed but unifying percussion background to the pops concert.

Now and then, the splash of a fish, probably a bass rudely reminded members of the frog fraternity that some residents of the lake marsh community prefer to dine on frogs rather than listen to their musical offering.

•

The voices of the night were mostly still when the first rays of the morning sun brightened the waters of the lake. Already another panorama began to unfold, featuring bird calls and insects amid beautiful scenery. Into such a setting came faithful long-time camp boosters, including Vaughn and Thelma Smith Marner of rural Meridian, and George and Ruby Birky Reno of Venice, Louisiana. Theirs was again the privilege of enjoying both daytime and nighttime performances of the many fascinating creatures at this lovely secluded campground in eastcentral Mississippi.

—August 10, 1978

The Most Brilliant of our Orchids

Look how the flowers grow;
they neither toil nor spin,
and yet, I tell you, even Solomon in all his grandeur
was never robed like one of them.
—Matthew 6:28-29

When I spotted the yellow fringed orchid, *Habenaria ciliaris*, while I was walking along the boardwalks at the Springville Marsh near Findlay, Ohio, recently, I was reminded of my first sighting of this orchid, one of the most beautiful wild flowers I have ever had the pleasure of meeting in its own native community. The color is really an orange-yellow, and the fringes on the petals give it an appearance of rare beauty, delicacy, and elegance.

In her 1899 book, *How to Know the Wild Flowers,* Mrs. William Starr Dana wrote, "Years may pass without our meeting the most brilliant of our orchids. Suddenly one August day we will chance upon just such a boggy meadow as we have searched in

Yellow fringed orchid:
lovely resident of grassy bogs

vain a hundred times, and will behold myriads of its deep orange, dome-like spires erecting themselves in radiant beauty over whole acres of land."

My first sighting of the gorgeous yellow fringed orchid growing in a damp area at Oak Openings Parks near Toledo in August 1982 was just such an exciting encounter as Mrs. Dana's book described.

•

Another elegant orchid, the nodding ladies' tresses, *Spiranthes cernua,* was also growing in the Springville fen when Bluffton College professor Richard Hansgen and I were observing the wildlife there several weeks ago. The white flowers of this orchid are arranged in a double spiral on a spike, resembling a Fourth-of-July sparkler with white sparks flying from the slender rod.

Back in 1942 when I was serving in the Civilian Public Service camp at Colorado Springs, my friend Ruth Parker gave me her copy of the Dana book on wild flowers. The book had been new when Miss Parker first used it to keep records of the plants she saw, jotting down date and place on the margins of the pages.

Beside the description of ladies' tresses, Miss Parker had noted: "Island of Nantucket, 4 Sept. 1900." I'm confident that this lovely flower delighted Miss Parker when she discovered it, as it thrilled me when I first met it on September 22, 1982, at Heritage Park, near Lima, Ohio—82 years later.

—October 8, 1992

Nature's Glory in the Heart of Dixie

Behold, to the Lord your God belong heaven and the heaven of heavens, the earth with all that is in it....
—Deuteronomy 10:14

Huge magnolia blossoms add to the scenery in much of the South. Next door to Kenneth and Mary Martin's family home in Brewton, Alabama, a handsome magnolia tree bears dozen of these beautiful flowers.

Thousands of insects, including some attracted to the magnolia blossoms, are consumed every day by a colony of purple martins tenanting a multi-apartment house on the Martin fenceline. The birds' continual chirping and chuckling radiates an atmosphere of a closely knit neighborhood. In flight, these large swallows artfully maneuver, not only in pursuit of prey,

Magnolia blossom, Brewton, Alabama

but, it appears, for the sheer enjoyment of exhibition flying.

•

At Burnt Corn Creek, near Brewton, David Blake, who knows the area well, led Kenneth and me through the moist lowland inhabited by cypress trees with their "knees" protruding from the muck.

On dryer ground, we found a mild-mannered gulf coast box turtle that when molested closes the hinged ends of its shell.

David also located what we tentatively identified as an eastern mud turtle. However, this species and the Mississippi mud turtle are thought to intergrade in that general area. The mud turtle also appeared meek, but there seems to be a disagreement as to its temperament. At any rate, this one showed no animosity toward us.

Mild in temperament, the gulf coast box turtle is a bashful creature. When handled, the turtle preferred to avoid our prying eyes by closing both the front and rear doors of its self-propelled habitation.

•

In the moist area of Burnt Corn Creek, we encountered a number of plants in bloom. A ruellia, perhaps the wild petunia of the South, was lovely. In muddy patches we found a wild iris with petals and sepals still wrapped in the bud.

Several widely distributed familiar plants included the black-eyed Susan, sneezeweed, and false dandelion.

•

David found a gray treefrog when he looked beneath a cardboard sign fastened to a tree. This small amphibian has tiny "suction cups" or adhesive discs at the tips of its toes, enabling it to cling easily to twigs and bark. Its call always reminds me of a hen quieting her chicks.

•

The parula warbler was in one of its favorite haunts, while the yellowhammer or flicker boldly called out as though proud that he is the state bird of Alabama.

•

Kenneth Martin, his little son Tim, and I spent a few delightful hours watching wildlife on the island of Santa Rosa near Pensacola, Florida.

Ruddy turnstones dawdled on the white sand, while a pair of least terns scolded us, apparently fearful of our presence too near their nest or young.

Many small sand crabs, blending almost perfectly with the white sand, moved cautiously in search of food washed in by the waves.

Once, an extremely wary crab sidled toward its den. At first it seemed to disappear into its tunnel. However, upon looking closely I saw a pair of black eyes, mounted on terminals, watching me from behind a ripple of sand. If I had not known of its presence, I would never have guessed that the little crab was people-watching.

Upon leaving the Brewton area I stopped to look at a beautiful bobcat that had been struck by an auto. Though saddened by its fate, I was made aware that some of these elegant bobcats still roam in Alabama, the heart of Dixie.

–August 24, 1978

Part IV

Autumn

Canada goose view of Springville Marsh

Those Who Make Homes in Marshes

Can the papyrus grow where there is no marsh?
Can reeds flourish where there is no water?
—Job 8:11

On a late September day, a small gang of Canada geese was loafing along the south shore of a lagoon at the Springville Marsh near Findlay, Ohio. Near that point, several common moorhens, *Gallinula chloropus*, slipped slowly through the reeds as though careful not to attract too much attention when venturing out into the open. At times, however, the moorhen acts quite tame, almost domesticated in some parks.

Back in 1946, I was surprised to see a moorhen dabbling about a garden pool in the countryside near Copenhagen, Denmark, its red frontal plates shining in the sunlight. In parts of Britain, the moorhen is known to be destructive to vegetables and fruit in kitchen gardens.

At times, the marsh hen constructs a nest that has a ramp of plant material. The nest is often able to rise or fall according to fluctuations of the water level, which is quite a feat of engineering, made even more awesome because there is no blueprint traced to guide its artful construction.

•

Sidney Lanier writes in *The Marshes of Glynn*:

As the marsh hen secretly
builds on the water sod,
Behold, I will build me a nest
on the greatness of God.
I will fly in the greatness of
God as the marsh-hen flies,
In the freedom that fills all
the space 'twixt the marsh
and the skies.

Lanier wrote this poem about a swampy area near the coast of Georgia in 1878. He probably observed the moorhens there as they went about crafting their nests. They work as a pair. Both also share the duty of incubation as well as caring for the awkward-looking downy youngsters.

•

Relaxing on a tussock surrounded by water, a spotted turtle quietly lay with a hind leg stretched out, letting the warmth of the bright autumn sunlight soak in. This species, *Clemmys guttata*, is reportedly rare. It is found at Camp Friedenswald in Michigan. The spotted turtle is a resident of marshes, bogs, and other shallow bodies of water.

•

As I walked the boardwalk in a drier area of the fen, I saw the shrubby cinquefoil, *Potentilla fruticosa*, whose bright yellow blossoms flashed from a background of the dark, moody muck. This is the same cinquefoil I have seen at the Rocky Mountain Mennonite Camp at an altitude of more than 9,000 feet.

The camp is in the subalpine belt, which reaches up to tree line. This cinquefoil or potentilla is the same species you may have in your yard. I was surprised to see it there in the marsh, brushing elbows with gentians and Kalm's lobelias, as well as several species of ferns.

•

An exquisitely colored snake glided effortlessly from its sunbathing pad on the boardwalk and slid into the water. Its back was a delicately blended fusion of rust and copper. Neither the snake nor I introduced ourselves. I often wish that I knew something more about the ways and still secret doings of this almost-gorgeous snake of Springville Marsh.

Continuing southward, I was delighted by a happy-go-lucky dragonfly that came bobbing along and lit for a thrilling second on my arm. It was a red one: delicate, yet amazingly structured, like a hang glider formed from firmly knit gauze.

As I walked on, a single-motored damselfly, slender, petite, and attired in flimsy blue, moved back and forth like a harrier on the prowl. Sunlight flashed from the delicately traced wings of this wandering beauty of the Springville Marsh.

—October 22, 1992

•

Several attractive ferns were plentiful on my visit to Springville Marsh. I saw many sensitive ferns, or bead ferns, *Onoclea sensibilis*, from the boardwalks. Their bead-like spore cases are held aloft on separate stems. The cases turn brown, making them conspicuous.

•

In the somber water nearby was a dwarf birch, *Betula pumila*, a tree I had never met before. Its hairy twigs hold small, toothed, oval leaves, which are soft on the surface.

Near the tree was a company of lovely fringed gentians, *Gentianopsis crinita*.

•

At the marsh, I was fortunate to observe Thomas Bartlett and his crew from the Ohio Deptartment of Natural Resources as they went about their bird-banding operation. They had suspended a half-dozen mist nets over various spots in the bog. Birds flew into these fine nets and were temporarily trapped. Tom's crew banded 31 birds that day.

Among the migrants was a very attractive mourning warbler with a blue-gray hood around its head and neck.

Another group of three or four warblers were American redstarts. They were on their way to Mexico, the West Indies, or perhaps some were traveling as far south as Peru and Brazil.

During the winters of 1947 and 1948, redstarts were not uncommon in Puerto Rico when we lived at Baranquitas. There they were called *candelitas*, or little candles. Their patches of orange and yellow on wings and tail flashed like little lights as they flittered about.

—October 8, 1992

Lake at Fellowship Point, Berne, Indiana

A Lovely Day at Fellowship Point

And God saw everything that he had made,
and behold, it was very good.
— Genesis 1:31

The lake at Fellowship Point, a site owned and operated by the First Mennonite Church of Berne, Indiana, was calm and lovely on that autumn day. Its clear water reflected some of the trees from the Howard and Bonnie Neuenschwander grove nearby.

Overhead, clouds of delicate texture moved softly and silently along as a great blue heron came winging in from the east. It banked sharply and landed when it saw me on the north shore where a colony of cattails would soon release their cottony covered seeds.

The heron had hardly landed before a mockingbird came in from the northeast, flying low and on a direct course to somewhere only it knew.

These musical mimics are not at all rare in the vicinity during the winter. One has been seen feeding on the yew and honeysuckle berries at Karl and Florence Hilty's home up until the middle of November or later. In the last Audubon Christmas Bird Count, 19 of the 24 Indiana counting groups reported them. This is not surprising since they were also being reported last winter from as far north as Pocatello, Idaho, Winnipeg, and southern British Columbia.

I hope some members of this jolly but hardy clan will stay around the area to delight birdwatchers and to surprise those who only associate the talented songsters with the deep South.

•

While Leonard (Boone) Whitehurst and I rambled over the interesting site at Fellowship Point we startled a cottontail which sped away, signaling a small company of song sparrows to hightail it for the nearest trees.

We also saw a single myrtle warbler, probably on its way southward. A blue jay announced its presence from an area called Hickory Knob. Later, the whining wings of a mourning dove broke the stillness as it took off from a nearby perch.

At Hickory Knob, shagbark and pignut hickories abound, to the delight of the fox squirrels whose nests are sometimes seen high in the trees.

A bunch of soft nesting material that we saw reminded my companion of the time he was mowing around the chapel at Fellowhip Point. After some

time he noticed a family of young mice and their mother cuddled in a nest beneath the riding seat of the mower. Perhaps the youngsters were not shaken up by the ride, but the mother must have been extremely loyal to risk the trip in order to stay with her offspring.

On another occasion Boone had watched a pair of Canada geese land on the lake, paddle up to shore and approach the chapel. The reflection in the glass doors disturbed the gander, who made no bones about how he felt when he thought another swain had invaded his territory.

•

A flock of about 200 Canadas has been observed at nearby Rainbow Lake and at Lake of the Woods. The large geese were a source of delight for Florence Hilty, Winifred Price, Naomi Augsberger, and other members of the Cardinal Chapter of the Audubon Society of Berne.

—December 9, 1976

Rest stop for migrating warbler

Warblers Range from Alaska to Panama

Thou makest springs gush forth in the valleys...
By them the birds of the air have their habitation;
they sing among the branches.
— Psalm 104:10,12

This warbler, possibly an immature myrtle, probably traveled quite a few miles before its rest stop at Bluffton. If a myrtle, its summer home may be in Canada, although some nest in Alaska. In winter, some migrate as far south as Panama.

The myrtle warbler is one of the most common of our warbler migrants. It is now called a form of yellow-rumped warbler; Audubon's warbler, farther west, is another form. The range quoted above is for the yellow-rumped warbler as a species.

While in Civilian Public Service near Colorado Springs, Colorado, I saw both forms of the yellow-rumped warbler in the same area at the same time. Audubon's has a yellow throat, while the myrtle has a white throat.

•

Warbler watching is great fun and brings much excitement to its participants, as is reflected in this poem written by Sonia K. Weaver when she was 12 years old. Sonia was birding with her parents and her sisters during the warbler migration. She was carrying a clipboard and had a pair of binoculars around her neck when she made these keen observations:

Flicker, Flit, and Flash

Standing in a tranquil woods,
Foliage surrounding me,
I see a little flitter
Darting quick from tree to tree.

No lack of fluttering feathers,
Birds in trees abound.
Jewels of the forest;
Warblers are all around.

Clusters of people smile
And exclaim in delight,
After sighting the warbler
Christened Black-and-White.
Flashing here, flitting there,

Like a flickering candle flame,
No two of these lively birds'
Bright colorings are the same.

Tiny wings are abundant,
The green is splotched with blue.
Scarlets, yellows, blacks are darting,
Periwinkles, too.

The woods have a rare and
simple beauty,
The growth is lush and green.
Those flashing, darting warblers
Are a pleasure to be seen!

What warbler watcher hasn't felt the same as Sonia did that day while birding at Crane Creek near Lake Erie in northern Ohio!

—May 28, 1981

Adventures of Raindrop, the Pet Mouse

Thou makest it dark;
night falls, and every wild beast in the wood is moving...
             —Psalm 104:20 (Moffatt)

Raindrop, a white-footed deer mouse, joined the household of Bob, Connie, and Wendi Gilliom of Berne, Indiana, in the fall of 1975. It happened when Nicky-the-Cat's bell awakened little Wendi, and she discovered Raindrop in the night-roving feline's clutches. Wendi's immediate reward for trying to rescue Raindrop was a nip from the tiny teeth of the wee mousie. Her cry for help aroused her mother, who dumped Raindrop into an old aquarium.

For a while, at least, Raindrop was safe from Nicky-the-Cat, who was no doubt disappointed that the tinkling bell had spoiled his fun. But he was a typical cat and was sure another opportunity would come. He was accustomed to biding his time.

•

Cozy in her pop can burrow lined with clothes-dryer lint, Raindrop contributed to the population explosion of the *Peromyscus* tribe by giving birth to a half-dozen blind and hairless babies. This occasion might not have been momentous for Raindrop, because deer mice reportedly bear from two to four litters a year.

Raindrop, the white-footed deer mouse

Fearing what a *Peromyscus* explosion might do in and around the house, and having little hope of finding homes for the young, the Gillioms "disposed of" the baby mice. This was done without the eager cooperation of Nicky-the-Cat, who probably had his own idea of how this type of situation could be solved by an ecologically sound procedure. Anyway, he still had his ideas about Raindrop and how to prevent the relatives of this meek mousie from inheriting the earth. He would wait; his time would come.

•

Raindrop, like Nicky-the-Cat, was a nocturnal animal, staying out of sight most of the day but scampering busily around at night.

The Gillioms furnished a rather elaborate cage — or should we say, "home" — for the white-stockinged beastie. There were intricate tunnels that would pass the most rigorous tests for safety and comfort. There was an excercise wheel that might well have been the envy of her outdoor relatives who were forced to exercise by hustling for daily bread and food for winter caches. For Raindrop, it seemed, the wheel was just a part of her elite lifestyle.

During the quiet of night, Raindrop kept trim by working the wheel for hours at a stretch. As it turned, a shrill squeaking compelled the Gillioms to file a family complaint against Raindrop for disturbing the peace. The case was settled out of court by transferring the Raindrop mansion to the bathroom. Nicky-the-Cat, however, was not consulted in the settlement, and his entry was barred by the closed door. But Nicky-the-Cat, like his forebears, was a patient hunter. He had time — lots of time.

•

Sumptuously dining on a gourmet's varied diet, the little *ratona*, I would assume, enjoyed a good life in contrast to her kinfolk roughing it in meadow and woods nearby. One of her favorite tidbits was chocolate M&M pillowettes. Carefully cracking the shell, Raindrop daintily nibbled the tasty filling, while her country cousins gnawed coarser fare.

However, like her untamed relatives, *Kla-tse-ha'na* of the Taos Indians and *Na-zon'-za* of the Navajos of far-away Arizona and New Mexico, Raindrop continually sought to escape. One night she managed to squeeze out of her mansion. But alas! Her freedom was short-lived, because Nicky-the-Cat quickly and professionally stalked and pounced upon the elfin escapee. Connie quickly rescued her, though, and wrote, "Nicky has a soft mouth; he knows if he bites too hard the mouse won't be able to play anymore. Mice are toys, not food!"

So both Raindrop and Nicky-the-Cat were disappointed. No freedom for the Indiana version of *Na-zon'-za*, and no one-sided play for the cat. But what neither knew was that Raindrop was soon to be transferred to Ohio and Nicky-the-Cat must seek elsewhere for his version of fun.

•

Raindrop, now at Bluffton, thrives on another varied diet. Sometimes we indulge her with black and English walnut meats that my brother Ray sent from Modesto, California.

Raindrop, however, is not yet free from cat surveillance. Our Ashley Ashford III (Ashes), like Nicky-the-Cat, seems fascinated by the sounds emanating from the cage. And Ashes, too, is patient—and waits.

—November 3, 1977

Along the Seashore at Acadia Park

Yonder is the sea, great and wide, which teems with things innumerable, living things both small and great.
—Psalm 104:25

The Acadia National Park in Maine is truly one of the most picturesque parks in our nation. The first national park established east of the Mississippi River, it includes about 32,000 acres on Mount Desert Island, Isle au Haut, and Schoodic Peninsula.

Foot trails connect various parts of the park where one

Mona Henry feeding the Herring Gulls at Acadia National Park, Maine

could spend weeks without re-tracing one's steps except at a few points. A system of good roads takes visitors to many scenic areas.

•

We visited a wonderful area called Schoodic peninsula at the recommendation of Merlin Groff, who lives in Augusta, Maine, with his wife Phyllis Bomberger Groff and their family. Merlin works for the Environmental Protection Agency and is acquainted with many areas of Maine. We were glad for his suggestion, because we found the peninsula extra-ordinarily interesting.

Our daughter Mona spent much time examining the sea-shore for sea shells. Shells of razor clams and blue mussels were plentiful along with peri-winkles, whelks, and barnacles. Mona also picked a green crab from the seaweed.

The razor clam, *Ensis directus*, closely resembles an old-fashioned razor case. By clamping its "foot" tightly against its shell, it can straighten out like a steel spring, propelling itself swiftly through the water. So if a clammer wishes to rinse his supply of razor clams in the water, he may suddenly find his whole catch disappearing while he stands amazed at the swift action of the supposedly sluggish shellfish.

•

We saw an eastern smooth green snake crossing the stony path at the top of Cadillac Mountain, which rises abruptly out of the sea to a height of 1,530 feet.

The beautiful snake, *Opheodrys vernalis*, is a very gentle reptile, living on the summit of the mountains along with golden-rod and flat-topped asters. Even at that height, bees and other insects visit the swaying flowering plants, seeking nectar and pollen just as the green snake looks for insects and spiders, the principal part of its diet.

•

American sea plantain flourished on the salt-sprayed beach at Winter Harbor, a part of Schoodic Peninsula. The plant is a relative of our buckhorn plantain that thrives too well in our lawns. *Plantago maritima*, however, probably prefers the beach to the ordinary garden plot.

The Nash sea lavender *Limonium nashii*, has long tapering stems covered (in August, at least) with many tiny pale purple blossoms, making quite an exciting show along the tidal flats.

Fireweed produces splashes of purplish-pink flowers in the meadows above the beaches. *Epilobium angustifolium*, with its four-petaled flowers, is a close relative of the evening primrose. These reminded me of my first delightful meeting with their kind at Camp Velaqua in Alberta, Canada, some years ago.

•

At Schoodic Point, the pink rocks were washed clean and bright by the receding waves. There a scattering of gulls became so bold that a few enterprising ones would approach a visitor and snatch pieces of bread from the person's outstretched hand. Sometimes the gulls would take food a person held high in the air. They presented a pretty picture as they gracefully hovered momentarily in midair, daintily accepting the tidbits.

I saw a few great black-backed gulls; they are more shy than the herrings. Several cormorants flew low over the water on a direct course, as though intent on serious business for the tribe.

As we left the point, Mona sighted a half grown porcupine scuttling into a ditch near the sea. Its innocent face was cute as it blinked at the onlookers. However, we did not attempt to cuddle the lovable looking animal, and we soon returned to our campsite at the Spruce Valley Campground on Desert Island after a day of fun and adventure.

—September 28, 1978

Long Awaited Rain in an Ohio Woods

Who can number the clouds by wisdom?
Or who can tilt the waterskins of the heavens,
when the dust runs into a mass and the clods cleave fast together?
— Job 38:37-38

The breaking of the long dry spell came very gently and quietly at first as a wavering line of scattered raindrops moved slowly across the thirsty field toward a small grove of hardwood trees.

Inside Ruth Welty's woods near Bluffton, only the soft caress of fine mist gave a hint that rain was falling. Leaning against the gray trunk of a huge beech, the observer could leisurely drink in the pungent musky aroma of the forest floor as it slowly dampened, releasing a delightful blending of incense.

Like the muffled tapping of a thousand typewriters, the sound intensified as raindrops fell faster and faster. Soon a few cupped leaves, soaked and filled with water, tipped one by one, pouring tiny cascades of rainwater onto the understory of shrubs and plants that lived on the forest floor.

•

From the edge of the woods, the hushed resonant note of a snowy tree cricket thumped out the temperature reading for anyone who knew the code.

The cricket soon ceased its "song" as the rain continued.

With the coming of the first hard frosts, the pleasant sound of the cricket would disappear until next year when its kin would unite with other musically-inclined insects in an orchestration whose concerts are a delightful part of summer's many offerings.

•

The low rumble of thunder reached the woods from somewhere to the south, quickly fading away like a squadron of jet planes speeding into the distance.

A single leaf, loosened by the pelting raindrops, drifted falteringly from the sheltering beech. The tempo of falling leaves quickened, the coppery blades managing a dulled sheen as they fell lightly through the grayness of the rainy woods.

•

Spider webs, strung and woven in the cavities of a decaying fallen tree, were made conspicuous by myriads of shattered raindrops that decorated the tiny threads.

In several webs were tiny crumbs of acorn cups and perhaps buckeye hulls, probably castoffs left by squirrels nibbling for goodies inside the hulls and shells.

The red berries of a clump of false Solomon's seal managed to shine in a quiet and modest manner even in the semidarkness of the dense canopy.

The green leaves of a sugar maple also reflected a bit of light from surfaces now thoroughly wet and slick.

As the rainfall slackened and came to a temporary halt, the plaintive, minor query of a tufted titmouse broke the sleepy monotony of the dripping woods. No answer came from others of its kin that might have been in the area.

•

Wild grapes at the fringe of the woods, sparingly washed by the downpour, had that tart and unique flavor that only such wild grapes possess. After a frost or two, the firm fruit would mellow and sweeten, if spared long enough by eager birds that have no compulsion to put off until tomorrow what is good enough to feast on today.

A yellow linden leaf sashayed down in silence from its mother tree somewhere near the border of the grove. It had hardly settled on the field where miniature rivers of clay-colored water tumbled into the crevices in the baked soil when a monarch butterfly fluttered heavily amid scattered raindrops. Flying southward it disappeared into the shelterbelt of trees along the creek.

•

Near the stream, in the deepening darkness a sodden thrush sought respite from the sudden downpour that had descended upon the forest again after a brief lull.

The thrush quickly began shaking out its soaked feathers, but then flew on a ways when it spied the intruder only a few yards away.

The cry of a blue jay sounded from along the field's edge as the steady shower continued to thoroughly drench the thirsty soil that had waited so long for this most welcome long-awaited rain.

—November 4, 1976

Leafboat and reflection on quarry waters

Tiny Ships Perform Fall Water Dance

Praise God forever! How he must rejoice in all his work!
—Psalm 104:31 (Living Bible)

The movement patterns among a flotilla of tiny ships on the glassy surface of the quarry were fascinating and unpredictable that day.

The first hard freezes of autumn had killed some leaves before leaf-fall. Many had dried and curled into various shapes. Some drifted onto the water or were blown there. Their many curiously formed sails fit them for active operation in myriads of ponds, lakes, marshes, and streams all over the country.

Many were the shapes, forms, and designs of such uncrafted ships maneuvering on the water. The dried leafboats reacted with amazing sensitivity to the faintest whiff of any autumn zephyr that stirred the quarry waters. They darted, spun, twirled, and danced crazily with amazing precision and sudden fits and starts, hesitations, and daring.

•

The arena for the maneuvers was a small nook on the west side of the quarry at Gratz's Spring Lake near Pandora, Ohio. Evidently the slight breezes and lazy water currents were spiraling and twirling, causing the tiny leafboats to pirouette about in a maddening, whirling-dervish manner.

As I lay on the bank of this natural arena, I was entranced by the gala maneuvers in progress only a few feet below me. I was loathe to leave the scene, for the performance was delightful and uniquely entertaining.

To think I've missed out on many such fascinating goings-on, which most anglers who fish from the bank of a stream or reservoir have no doubt witnessed many times. Or perhaps fishers, too, often fail to enjoy these exciting performances because of the rapt attention given to bobber or taut fishline drifting in the midst of the cavorting leafboats.

Anyway, I'm glad I stopped to relax and watch the silent drama that early evening while camping near Gratz's spring-fed quarry.

•

One morning recently, a tiny golden fan lay in the mud a few rods from Riley Creek just west of the National Quarry. The pattern and color of the ginkgo leaf caught my attention, for I was not aware that a mother tree bearing such uniquely designed leaves was in the area.

The ginkgo, *Ginkgo biloba*, is found on the Bluffton College campus and in several other parts of town, but I had never noticed one in the vicinity where the leaf was plastered in the mud. I later found many other leaves near the same spot, so will try to locate the tree that bore the fanlike leaves.

The ginkgo tree belongs to an ancient group whose fossils have been found on many continents. The ginkgo seems to have survived in China for centuries. I'm glad some of that stock found its way to our country.

•

While walking the dam at the National Quarry recently, I noticed many splotches of bright green lichens on the bark of some of the trees. The recent rain and days of moisture saturated air must have been just what the lichens and mosses needed after a dry summer.

—November 28, 1991

Experiences with Gulls and Coots

And God said, "...let birds fly above the earth across the firmament of the heavens."
                                        —Genesis 1:20

Ring-billed gull and coot

Migrant coots and ring-billed gulls are among the many birds that panhandle during the winter at MacArthur Park in Los Angeles, California.

Rafts of coots along with many ducks, mainly scaup, a scattering of ring-necks, and a few ruddys, apparently adapt well to the presence of park visitors and the noise of nearby traffic. A small flock of ringed turtle-doves, mourning doves, and other birds also frequent the park in winter and some are present there throughout the year.

It would be good to be in L.A. again for their annual bird count, in which I was privileged to participate December 28, 1975.

Among the 147 species tallied by 97 observers were nine species of gulls, with the ring-billed being the most numerous. Our party was confined to the Griffith Park area—a good place for birders at any time of the year.

•

An interesting experience with a coot, or mud hen, took place in Kansas many years ago.

A group of grade school children from the Moundridge community and their teacher encircled a small weed patch on the dried beach of Lake Inman. We had watched a coot enter the clump and were determined to see it up close.

After scanning the small patch for some time we felt a bit foolish when we could not see the bird. Finally we sighted a red eye shining from the greenery. After I caught the coot, each child enjoyed the experience of stroking its smooth back and fluffy sides.

Upon being released, the mud hen headed for the lake where it was no doubt relieved to have "escaped" from the band of curious children.

•

The trusting nature of Franklin's gulls was demonstrated one day on Sam and Hilda Hiebert Ratzlaff's farm near Hillsboro, Kansas.

As I recall Sam's account of the incident, a gull was gliding a few feet above his head as he drove the tractor pulling the corn lister. Sam decided to try his luck at grabbing the gull. He was probably surprised when he succeeded in plucking the sleek bird from the air.

After showing the bird to his family, Sam released it to continue its search for grubs, earthworms, and field mice as it followed the turning of the soil.

•

Tossing white grubs into the air for gulls to grab was fun when I was a young boy in Kansas. When a grub was thrown into the air, the gulls, seemingly without effort and with very little movement, adroitly plucked the offering and continued gliding along.

As the horsedrawn plow driven by my father or one of my older brothers turned larvae up, a flock of Franklin's gulls followed. The buoyant birds barely touched the moist, sweet-smelling earth as they picked up the grubs and other squirming tidbits. The gulls were amazingly tame and would often hover a few feet above the head of the driver and the barefoot boy following in the furrow.

•

Gulls that follow the plow and lister have quite a system of using the air currents as they glide and hover above freshly turned soil.

One time when I was plowing on the Bethel College farm at North Newton, Kansas, a flock of Franklin's gulls trailed behind. The wind was from the south, so they headed southward as the tractor went in that direction. When we reached the south end of the field, the gulls wheeled and flew directly nonstop to the north end. There they turned, again headed into the wind, and resumed hovering and sailing slowly across the field, using the south wind to buoy them up as they leisurely scanned the soil below.

Whether the gulls are migrating to northen U.S. or the prairies of southern Canada in the spring or to the Pacific Coast of Central or South America in the fall, it's always a treat for Kansans who happen to spot the birds when they stop to rest and feed along the way.

–December 8, 1977

Water Bugs That Dive, Whirl, Skate

And God said, "Let the waters bring forth swarms of living creatures...."
So God created every living creature that moves, with which
the waters swarm.... And God saw that it was good.

— Genesis 1:20-21

Predaceous diving beetle

This sleek and shiny diving beetle was found one autumn as it flew to an outdoor light at Ralph and Wilma Stern's Bluffton home.

Upon seeing the beetle, with its wings an iridescent color and its stylish design, Wilma described it as resembling a brooch.

Dytiscus marginalis has a body so perfectly formed for underwater movement that it should be the envy of those persons who don diving suits for recreation or underwater research.

The beetle's wings are fashioned so that it is able to carry a supply of air with it as it travels underwater. The beetle's hind legs are also equipped with bristles that aid its submarine maneuvers.

Its larvae, called "water tigers," prey on small underwater animals. During the winter the adults stay buried in the mud. Certain adult members of the water beetle family are used for food and medicine in parts of the Orient.

The predaceous diving beetles may be dangerous not only to aquatic insects, but also to frogs, snails, tadpoles, and other animals found in water.

In some fish hatcheries, these diving beetles can cause considerable loss of small fish. However, their own eggs are often parasitized by at least four species of tiny wasps that enter the water to seek them out. Their larvae are also attacked by certain thread worms, while adults are readily eaten by ducks, frogs, and other predators.

The beetle only stores about 20 minutes worth of air under its wings, yet it can stay down for almost 36 hours. This is because as the air is used, the oxygen pressure inside the bubble of air lowers, enabling oxygen from the surrounding water to diffuse into the bubble, which in this case acts like a gill.

Another interesting fact about the diving beetle is that experiments indicate that they are sensitive to sour, sweet, salt, and bitter, just as human beings are.

A further fascinating fact is that they, along with a number of other insects, have their hearing organs on their tarsi, the "tippie toes" of their legs. In such an arrangement, a case of tired feet would probably cause hearing loss. So it must be fortunate for them that "treading water" is probably easier on their ears than walking on land.

•

The bright and shiny "bugs" we often see in great numbers whirling around on water surfaces are whirligig beetles. How they manage to cavort about in such great numbers without crashing into one another is a wonder.

Perhaps the whirligig beetles do not bump into each other because of their unique organs of sight. Each of their compound eyes is divided into two parts: one part stays dry and the other remains underwater. The two pairs must come in mighty handy, for while one pair scans the heavens, the other can watch the goings-on of the underwater world.

This beetle can also dive, carrying a bubble of air with it as it goes under water.

It feeds upon insects, dead or alive, that touch the surface of the water. The whirligigs are also important in the diets of water birds and fishes.

Some species may secrete a milky fluid that has the odor of ripe apples.

•

The water strider is an aquatic bug with which most of us are familiar. We see them skating on the water, making little dimples on the shiny surface as they go.

When we were children in Kansas, we wondered how they found their way to our stock tanks. We never saw them fly as we tried to capture them, but authorities say that some adults have wings, while others do not.

We noticed that when a water strider was forced beneath the water, it would pop up instantly. This is because its legs and body are clad in dense velvety pile.

Water striders live on insects that fall onto the water's surface. They are also scavengers.

—September 23, 1982

Heard Any Caterpillars Lately?

He has caused his wonderful works to be remembered....
— Psalm 111:4a

Black locust borer beetle

The adult of the black locust borer is a handsome beetle with transverse and oblique bands accented against its velvety black body.

I first encountered this dashing beetle at Camp Friedenswald in Michigan several Septembers ago. It was dining on goldenrod pollen. This beastie lays its eggs under the scales of black locust bark. Later, its eggs hatch into larvae that make their living feeding on the bark. They later enter the wood. The black locust borer's eating habits can do great damage to the tree that it infests.

When I first found this beetle, I was unaware that it was able to emit sounds. Just recently at the Wilderness Center near Wilmot, Ohio, a member of our prairie scouting group caught one. As she held it in her cupped hands the beetle made a series of barely audible sounds. Later I captured one that also sounded off, either in protest or perhaps in fright. Anyway, it was quite a surprise to hear a beetle reacting in this way when held captive.

•

Another beetle is the milkweed beetle, *Tetraopes femoratus*. When held between finger and thumb, this attractive pink colored beetle bends at the juncture of the thorax and abdomen. Perhaps this buckling is what causes the barely audible squeaks that emanate from the beetle.

Although these attractive beetles do not make music as lively as that of the katydids, crickets, and cicadas, perhaps to these beetles their efforts produce sounds every bit as pleasant as those of the better-known members of the insect summer orchestra.

•

Have you heard any caterpillars lately?

According to *The Insect Guide*, by Klots and Klots, many sphinx caterpillars squeak, and larvae of various skipper butterflies produce grating sounds when they scrape their jaws over a leaf surface. Even the pupae of certain butterflies make noise by scraping their abdominal segments together, or at least that is the report we get from some caterpillar watchers. For myself, I had never thought to listen to caterpillars, until I read Klots. Even now, the thought of trying to eavesdrop on a caterpillar appears to be quite a challenge and a rather humbling experience for those of us who take delight in listening to our songbirds and the orchestration of insect musicians. So the next time you pick up a wiggly, woolly caterpillar, lend it an ear; perhaps it will reward you with a squeak or some other sound of greeting or protest.

•

Have you listened to any butterflies or moths recently? Surely, you may respond, bees and mosquitos may hum and crickets may fiddle, but moths—you must be kidding! But *The Insect Guide* again informs us that there is more sound out there in a quiet afternoon than we ever dreamed possible.

The book states that the adults of the death head moth can produce a high-pitched sound by forcing air through their mouths. The whistling moth of Australia gets its common name from the sound made by adult males during courtship. This is done with a hollow membrane of the wings.

After you gain some success at hearing the sound of moths and butterflies, you may become bold enough to approach your neighbor and say, "I heard butterflies today!" If so, you will probably be given a strange, furtive look before your neighbor quickly walks away, shaking his head in disbelief and puzzlement. But do not give up; perhaps, by and by, there will be as many devoted butterfly-listeners as there are those who enjoy the songs of birds and crickets.

—October 14, 1982

Blue-stemmed goldenrod

Surprising Plants Offer Marvelous Motion

Thou visitest the earth and waterest it...
the valleys deck themselves with grain,
they shout and sing together for joy.
　　　　　　　　—Psalm 65:9,13

Walking along the Bluffton Quarry some weeks ago, I was glad to see my first goldenrod starting to bloom this season. Others, I'm sure, were already in blossom, but this early beauty caught my attention.

The attractive blue-stemmed goldenrod, *Solidago caesia,* I know only from a colony growing in the college cabin area on the nature preserve here at Bluffton. Alison Deckert Hiebert called my attention to a scattering of these "wreath" goldenrods about 10 years ago. Neither of us has seen this species at any other site since then.

The common name of this plant comes from the blue-gray flush on the stems. *Solidago* refers to the curative qualities of the goldenrods, *caesia* to the bluish-gray of the stalks.

•

Several species of goldenrod are known to produce good tea from their dried leaves. A special one is the sweet goldenrod, *S. odora*, which shows transparent dots on the leaves. When crushed, they exude the aroma of anise.

Another species, the Missouri goldenrod, *S. missouriensis*, not only makes a good tea, but the young greens are used as a pot-herb. The dried leaves are some-times powdered and used as an antiseptic. By boiling the stems and leaves, an antiseptic lotion can be made.

•

During the dry spell we had recent-ly in our area, I was watering a dwarf hydrangea by our porch. As I knelt beside it, out of the corner of my eye I noticed a movement among the foliage. Curious, I began to watch the plant for other movements, finally I caught a leaf in the act of pop-ping into position. Then I spied another—and yet another. I was excited! For the first time ever, I was witnessing a plant rearranging its foliage just as a bird may fluff out its feathers after a shower.

It appeared that the thirsty soil was ravenously sucking up the moisture while the plant roots were greedily absorbing it. As water filled the stems and leaves, they became turgid, resuming their natural healthy forms. The drama was a brand new performance for me. I was awed to see it happening before my eyes. Amazing! Marvelous!

This drama was just a hint of what a writhing sea of motion must take place when a whole field of corn or sorghum is drink-ing in water from a much-needed rain. The apparent calm and quiet of such a field must be se-cretly woven with the whisperings of thousands of plants joining to lift and lightly caress perked-up leaf-blades in common praise of a welcome rain.

—September 23, 1993

Drifting Away on Gossamer Thread

...his trust is a spider's web.
—Job 8:14

Autumn features an array of giant webs woven by the large orange-and-black garden spiders, *Argiope aurantia*, at times known as *A. riparia*. Sometimes the huge silken orbs stretch several feet, reaching from one anchor point to another.

Oftentimes while moving along a trail we run smack-dab into one of these wheel-and-spoke webs spanning the path. When they have no dew clinging to them, the nets are almost invisible, and we are surprised by our collisions with the resilent webbing of the tough insect traps.

Our black-and-yellow *Argiope* is beautifully arrayed with bright yellow markings on a black background. This is one of the most conspicuous garden spiders in our area.

The striped or banded garden spider is another strikingly marked one. Its abdomen has a background of white or light yellow crossed by a series of black transverse lines. *Argiope transversa*, as well as *A. aurantia*, are fascinating residents of the Bluffton College Nature Preserve.

•

One early morning recently, Harvey and Alison Deckert Hiebert took a walk in the Bluffton College Nature Preserve. Harvey said the vegetation was covered with dew, and so were the myriads of spider webs blanketing the grasses and other plants. When vegetation is viewed across a dewy meadow, the hundreds of orb and sheet webs present a gossamer landscape that is indeed breathtaking.

Such scenes are most often viewed during late summer and early autumn, especially during a spell of Indian summer. By then,

Giant spider waits for a catch

most web weavers are mature, and their ingenious handiwork dew-covered in the morning. Our Indian summer has also been known as gossamer goose summer: "season of goose and cobwebs."

•

When we were children on the farm in Gypsum Valley of Saline County, Kansas, we would sometimes chase a parachute of gossamer as it floated along in the autumn breeze. Often we found a spider nonchalantly sailing along on the clump of webbing drifting with the wind.

Along the roadsides during the season of drifting gossamer, we can see thousands of shiny threads dangling from utility lines, barbed wire fences, and hedges. With the autumn morning sunlight reflecting from the silvery drapery, the scene can be spectacular.

Just what species of spider uses this method of traveling to new sites I haven't discovered. At times, however, I have watched a spider, stationed on top of a fence post, spinning threads of gossamer that were floating outward with the autumn breeze. No anchor point was seen for the threads to contact. Perhaps after a while, there would be enough material to lift the spider up like a silver balloon, carrying the adventurer into the bright blue yonder. Wonderful!

•

In the lawn of our farm yard in the Gypsum Valley, we often discovered the entrances to the vertical burrows of the wolf spider. We children would pour water down the burrow and capture the large arachnids when they surfaced.

Female wolf spiders drag their egg sacs, fastened to their spinnerets, along the ground. When the spiderlings emerge, they clamber on the mother's back, riding until they are mature enough to dismount and go hunting on their own.

I have often seen the large females dragging their egg sacs through stubble in a field while I was plowing or at harvest time. Sometimes they had their little offspring riding piggy-back without saddle or stirrups—bareback, that is.

I have also seen smaller species of wolf spiders high in the Rocky Mountains, on the tundra above the treeline. I have watched the white egg sacs trace a trail through the hardy grasses as the mother spiders dragged the sacs along at an altitude of more than 11,000 feet. Intriguing!

—October 14, 1993

Third Graders Spot Bugs, Odd Squirrel

And I will make for you a covenant that day with the beasts of the field, the birds of the air, and the creeping things of the ground....
—Hosea 2:18

Several weeks ago, Cheryl Althaus, a teacher at the Pandora-Gilboa Elementary School at Pandora, Ohio, brought her third grade class to the Bluffton College Nature Preserve. That morning, though cold, turned out to be a beautiful and exciting one.

Half of the class went exploring with Cheryl and with naturalist Alison Deckert Hiebert. Their group soon met up with a single large milkweed bug—a

Large milkweed bug

brightly-colored red, orange, and black bug that frequents milk-weed plants, dining on their seeds. The cold weather had driven most of them into hiding. Only a few weeks ago, other third graders had seen dozens gathered in milkweed colonies at the preserve.

Our team failed to spot any of the milkweed bugs on our walk, but afterwards I met up with a brilliant loner sunning itself on a weathered pod. Probably still others would emerge as the day warmed up from a late October sun.

•

Earlier in the autumn, our hikers sometimes manage to spot another colorful insect, the red longhorn milkweed beetle. This is perhaps *Tetraopes tetrophthalmus*, one of about 28 species of this genus found in North America.

If held between the forefinger and thumb, the beetle emits a bare-ly audible squeak of protest, perhaps caused by rubbing togeth-er rough areas of the thorax. Anyway, it is a test to see how keenly our young hikers can hear.

The red longhorn milkweed beetle is a soft pinkish-red with several distinct black spots adorn-ing its slick uniform.

The eyes are divided, making four instead of the usual two— the upper and lower portions widely separated. "The better to see you with, my dear," might well be the reason for this. Our beetle, at the slightest hint of danger when people are snooping into its lifestyle pattern, executes a simple getaway maneuver: it drops to the sod and quickly disappears.

Adult red longhorn milkweed beetles feed on milkweed and are immune to the poison of its juice. Larvae bore into stems and roots of the plant. The larvae are poisonous to birds.

•

A third grader in my group loudly called attention to a white squirrel fleeing off into the distance. We later saw it for a few moments near the swinging bridge across from the college cabin. However, it again disappeared among the trees, but not before we noted its small size, suggesting a little red squirrel. We did not, of course, have a chance to see its eyes, which should have been pink if a true albino. Anyway, it was a great surprise and unexpected bonus for the members of my group.

•

An interesting coincidence occurred when we paused outside one of our nature center buildings where I mentioned the possiblility of a winter nature walk. I recalled that once, while on a winter walk, we had seen dozens of meadow mice or voles when the snow was deep and the voles active even in daytime. At that moment a vole appeared at a corner of the building as though programmed to entice the children to plan for a winter walk. A minute or two later, it reappeared. This time Joyce Ginther, driver of the school bus, noticed the vole and called it to the attention of some of the pupils who had missed its brief appearance the first time.

Probably for most of the children, this was their first sighting of the cute, white-tummied, bob-tailed, short-eared vole, but for me it was a reminder of Peter-the-Prairie-Vole we had as a pet while living at Pekin, Illinois, some years ago.

So once again an unexpected sighting added special excitement to a late-October nature walk.

−November 26, 1987

Brothers Hiked in California Ranges

I lift up my eyes to the hills.
From whence does my help come?
My help comes from the Lord, who made heaven and earth.
        −Psalm 121:1-2

This little tyke sits in the cup of an acorn from a canyon live oak and still has room to spare, for this froggie measures only one to two inches in length. However, whenever it decides to hop, look out! The accomplished broad-jumper escaped several times during a photo session in which he kept his captor hopping.

At one point, the tiny frog disappeared through the grill of

California treefrog in acorn cup

a car. It took some maneuvering to get him to slip out into the open where I could recapture him.

His leaps at times covered from three to four feet, and the tiny suction cups on his toes enabled him to alight on a wall and stick fast, duly anchored by the efficient little adhesive disks.

•

My brother Ralph found the treefrog when he and I were returning to the highway in the Tijunda Canyon last October. A stream of very cold water was trickling along the arroyo we were scrambling up. Suddenly Ralph called out that he saw a toad in a little pool along the arroyo. I answered that he should capture it if he could. Soon he had the little fellow in his hand. I saw by the miniature suction cups on its toes that it was a member of the treefrog family.

After arriving at the house, I readily identified the little frog as a California treefrog, which was a new species to me. I was delighted and soon made plans to take a number of black and white photos if I could get the tiny one to sit still a moment or two at a time.

Hyla cadaverina is common in suitable habitats in various parts of California. Ralph and I noticed its color change according to where placed it.

•

Regular readers of "Wayside Revelations" have probably noticed that I often refer to my brother Ralph, whose home was in Montrose, California. On January 4, 1985, he passed away unexpectedly at his home.

Ralph and I had tromped a number of times in the foothills and mountains of the San Gabriels. He and I had also hiked in the San Bernadino and San Jacinto mountains in southern California.

Just this past September and October, we made at least a half dozen treks into the San Gabriels. Ralph was probably at least as well acquainted with the San Gabriels as any other person. He hiked in the foothills, canyons, and the higher reaches of the mountains, collecting stones and transporting choice polished rocks to his home by bicycle and automobile.

As a partner in hiking, Ralph was interested in all beautiful and interesting things. He appreciated trees and shrubs, marveling at the huge incense cedars of the higher altitudes in the San Gabriels. He would hike an extra mile in rough country to measure a huge California alder he knew was out there beside a cold stream. He seemed interested in everything I happened to stop to investigate or admire, and was very patient with my many pauses to take photos or scrutinize a plant along the trail.

Ralph will be missed in a special way as I continue to hike in the San Gabriels. I will miss his familiar, "Come here, Roy; isn't this pretty!"

—*January 24, 1985*

Mid-autumn snow

Snow, Birds Herald Winter's Approach

Have you entered the storehouses of the snow,
or have you seen the storehouses of the hail?
                    —Job 38:22

"This is the first soft snow that tiptoes up to your door."
                    —May Sarton

Slowly the gray doorstep is dappled by splotches of soft snow as an airy brush artfully sweeps puffs of fluff and silken glitter over the threshold. Quietly, inexorably, the leaden color disappears—a twinkling white coverlet now lies snugly before the door.

Later, the cushioned steps are marred by faint, jagged shadows of outlines pressed out by a pair of retreating boots. Soon, the insistent snow renews the flowing grace of the thickening pad as the tiptoeing returns again and again.

The autumn landscape is now changed forever. The snow is falling. Let it fall, quietly, gently, serenely. This is northwestern Ohio in mid-November.

•

The trees along the dike display tufts of cotton, as the autumn snow snuggles between twig and branch, sketching dark "V" designs against a cold, gray sky. Dark stumps are now capped by a layer of soft, thick, white frosting.

The quarry's leaden waters are enlivened by a hundred or so Canada geese, comfortably bobbing on the smooth, lightly swelling cushion. A scattering of mallard ducks hardly seems to notice a large herring gull sweeping down among them, dipping the surface for some floating morsel, then rising, flying up and out and away for whatever reason it has to do so. Moments later, it repeats the same routine.

Within minutes, out of the gray, low-hanging sky, scores of black-tipped wings appear as if by magic, noiselessly, indistinct. Even moments later, still almost fairy-like, the new birds join the lone gull patrolling the quarry. Ducks and geese now take notice—calmly aware. Amid the hush of the hour and the gentle falling snow, the quarry becomes truly alive.

•

Near the western shoreline, a great blue heron adds movement to the scene as it awkwardly seeks out a safer perch at the water's edge. A lone kingfisher, cackling erratically, zigzags from nowhere to nowhere—or so it appears to the somewhat arrogant nonkingfisher, who is ignorant of the intricate flight path calculations of the professional spearfisher.

Through scattered hardwoods between Riley Creek and the quarry, a dark, blurred suggestion of a bird torpedoes into view for a slight arcing moment, defying instant recognition by the inquisitive biped. Hazarding a guess from past experience, I suggest that the shadowed projectile glimpsed on the flawed scanner is possibly a song sparrow.

As I look down on Riley Creek, the stream seems narrower to me. Stretching from shoreline outward over the quieter waters, a hidden film of ice is betrayed by a tell-tale blanket of soft snow.

My attention is soon drawn to a murmuring quintet of puddle ducks contentedly dipping and grubbing around the shallow waters where the hard-nosed current strongly disallows ice-making there for the present.

This first snowfall puts a new perspective to autumn in mid-November here at Bluffton and throughout northwest Ohio.

•

At home, flashes of iridescence call my attention to a foursome of cowbirds—males, that drop in for a quick lunch at the feeder-bar. On their hurried way southward, the handsome buffalo birds do not hang around long to discuss the weather. They are probably adequately attuned to what prospects lie ahead as they journey toward warmer parts of the country.

A sleek, red-breasted nuthatch dashes in to snatch a slippery sunflower seed. It, too, doesn't wait around to bid the time of day or comment on the first soft snow of autumn. This is the first visit by a member of its clan this season. Its white-breasted cousin, however, has already spied out the prospects for a fall and winter supply source and has become a rather common daily visitor.

A titmouse also stops by for a spell, looking quite tart and tufted as it cocks its bespeckled head to survey the feed offering. By and by, a thoroughly gorgeous redbird leisurely surveys the feed-bar. The redbird then takes its own sweet time to shell squash seeds left especially for such a connoisseur of rare foods and elegant finery. Autumn is quickly passing—winter cannot be far behind.

—*December 14, 1991*